Acknowledgments

Several people have contributed to the completion of this book. I begin by thanking all of the parents who have worked hard with me over the years learning the techniques to help their children develop friendships and social skills. They have tested many of the concepts and procedures presented in this book. I acknowledge Beth Doll who introduced me to the idea that parents should be involved in social skills training for children, and Candace Dee, Rob Jones, Wayne Binns, and Brett Wilson who assisted in developing some of the themes. I also thank several individuals who have helped pilot this and related works, including Dorlene Walker, Jaqui Richard, Kelly Stout, Angela Swanson, and Tamara Stratton.

Why Don't They Like Me?
Helping Your Child Make and Keep Friends

Susan M. Sheridan, Ph.D.

Edited by Francelia Sevin
Cover and Text Layout/Design by Tracy Katzenberger
Cover and Inside Illustrations by Suzanne Gebhardt
Production Assistance by Kimberly Harris

ISBN 1-57035-124-4

Printed in the United States of America

Published and Distributed by

SOPRIS
WEST

4093 Specialty Place   Longmont, CO 80504   (303) 651-2829
www.sopriswest.com

25LIKEME/3-03/KEN/1M/272

Dedication

To the hundreds of parents, including my own, who have put in countless hours to help their children develop better social skills. Their efforts, experiences, and stories are reflected in this book and will assist hundreds of other parents in doing the same for their children.

About the Author

Susan M. Sheridan, Ph.D., is a professor of educational psychology at the University of Nebraska, Lincoln. Her primary research interests are in the areas of social skills intervention and generalization, home-school partnerships, parent involvement, and consultation with parents and teachers of students with social, behavioral, and academic difficulties. She has published several books, chapters, and journal articles on these and related topics. Dr. Sheridan is the author of *The Tough Kid Social Skills Book*, published by Sopris West. She also conducts workshops and other professional development activities nationally.

Since the late 1980s, Dr. Sheridan has worked with children and parents to help children develop appropriate social skills and abilities to get along well with others. She has conducted groups for children and parents, and continues to lead or supervise groups in clinic and school settings. Dr. Sheridan is also active in professional organizations, including Division 16 (School Psychology) of the American Psychological Association; the National Association of School Psychologists; and the Utah Association of School Psychologists. She was named Utah School Psychologist of the Year in 1996, Outstanding Young Alumnus from the University of Wisconsin—Madison in 1995, and was honored with the prestigious Lightner Witmer Award for early career accomplishments from Division 16 of APA in 1993.

Preface

The information contained in this book was compiled over several years as a direct result of working with parents of children who had difficulties making and keeping friends. Over the past 8-10 years, I have worked with many parents to help them learn strategies for teaching their children social skills. The strategies in this book have been tried, tested, and revised in order to identify the strategies that are most effective. What is contained in this book are the skills that seem to be the most important for parents and children.

Parents generally want what is best for their children, and they want to help their children. A common difficulty that many parents report, however, is that they do not know what they can do to help their children. This book was written to give parents tools and techniques to assist children in developing better social skills. The skills, examples, and situations are all taken from actual reports provided by parents and their children. By applying the procedures outlined in this book, many parents and children have been able to learn important skills that can be used over time as children's needs change. Parents have reported that these procedures are invaluable in helping to develop a framework for talking to their children about friendship problems, and for encouraging their children's social skill use in everyday situations. In fact, in a study conducted using this model, parents demonstrated clearly that they can learn and use the skills in everyday interactions with their children (Sheridan, Dee, Morgan, McCormick, & Walker, 1996).

In working with parents over the years, I have learned that it is not only desirable for parents to learn skills to help their children learn and use appropriate social skills, it is necessary. A study focusing on helping children with withdrawn behaviors use appropriate initiation skills (such as asking others to play or starting a conversation) found that when parents were involved, children increased the use of these skills at home. When only school personnel were involved, however, the children used the skills only at school, not at home (Sheridan, Kratochwill, & Elliott, 1990).

Another lesson learned in working with parents is that these strategies do not work on their own. Just having the information is not enough; parents have reported that, through consistent use and trial-and-error, major changes in children's social relationships have been seen. But it takes work, time, and patience. The positive effects of this effort are not only improved social behavior on the part of children, but also improved parent-child relationships. The procedures presented in this book can make an important difference in your life, and the life of your child. What is most important is that constant and sincere efforts be made to use the strategies, and that you stick with it. Keep trying—you and your child are worth it!

Contents

Appendix (cont'd)

Introduction

How Do I Use This Book?

All children have problems with friends. And, all parents want what's best for their children. But not everyone knows what to do when problems arise, or how to best help children when they need it. As the name implies, this book will help parents help their children make and keep friends. If you follow the general guidelines and procedures covered in this book, your child will learn important skills to get along better with others. And you will likely develop a better relationship with your child.

This book is designed to provide parents with strategies to help children deal with difficulties with friends, classmates, and others. Specific social skills are reviewed, and techniques that parents can use to support their children as they learn are presented.

The procedures that are introduced in this book to help you teach and reinforce social skills (such as coaching, reminding, and talking to your child) can be applied at any age level, from preschool through middle school and beyond. Many of the examples provided and the words suggested to convey ideas to your child are centered around the middle elementary ages (ages 7-13). However, with minor adjustments, these ideas can be conveyed meaningfully to an older or younger child. What is most important is that the examples you use are realistic for your child (and you know your child better than anyone!), and that you use language that your child will understand. Chapter 1 is an overview of social skills. Problems children have with friends are discussed. Differences between children who are shy or who do not play much with others, and those who act out or fight with others are described. Although these types of children are quite different from each other, both are in need of social skills training. The important role that parents play in helping their children is also discussed in Chapter 1, setting the stage for the remainder of the book.

Chapter 2 describes the skills children need in order to get along with others. These include social entry skills (Getting Started), such as reading and using body language, starting conversations, joining in games and conversations, and talking about feelings. Social entry skills are necessary to make friends and to set up positive interactions.

Skills that maintain friendships and positive interactions (Keeping It Going), including keeping a conversation going and playing cooperatively, are also explored. Finally, skills for Solving Problems, including controlling anger, dealing with teasing, handling being left out, and accepting "no," are presented. All children find themselves in difficult situations at times. Steps for dealing with difficult situations help children to adjust and solve problems.

Chapter 3 provides step-by-step procedures by which you can help your child learn social skills. Procedures include coaching, showing, practicing, and reinforcing. Steps for helping your child set goals and for developing social skills contracts are highlighted.

In Chapter 4, specific strategies are presented for encouraging your child to use social skills. These include reminding your child to use skills "on the spot" when playing with others, and supporting friendships. An important part of learning social skills is being able to practice them, so providing opportunities for your child to play with others and talking to him/her about friends are necessary. In each of the chapters, you will find examples, suggestions, and "how-to" steps to help you understand social skills and guide you through the simple methods provided. Checklists for talking to your child, coaching, reminding your child to use appropriate social skills, practicing skills, and drawing up a contract are included in the Appendix.

This book is meant to provide general guidelines, procedures, and tools. You are encouraged to use the book in a way that is most sensible and useful to *you*. Your first step might be to review the skills presented in Chapter 2. Based on your observations and knowledge of your child, select those skills that are most important. Start with some basic skills and build up to more difficult ones. If your child seems to catch on quickly, feel free to move along. Or, if your child seems to need more time reviewing or practicing certain skills, take the time he/she needs. After teaching one or two skills (using the procedures covered in Chapter 3), it might be a good idea to jump ahead to Chapter 4 and review how to assist your child to use the skills in everyday situations.

You will find Social Skills Cards in the back of this book that provide step-by-step "recipes" for teaching social skills. A study by Colton and Sheridan (in press) found using small "recipe cards" to be an effective technique for teaching social skills. The cards can be removed easily from the book and can be carried with you and referred to when you are working on a skill with your child. The cards contain information about the skill being taught (i.e., skill steps), suggestions for what to emphasize (Do's and Don'ts), ideas for showing your child what the skill looks like, and situations that you might consider having your child practice. You may find it helpful to cover the cards with clear plastic recipe card covers, which you can find in most kitchen stores. This will protect them and allow you to refer to them often. You might even consider posting the card in a visible place to serve as a frequent reminder to you and your child about the skills that you are working on. You will have lots of opportunities to use these tools, and to help your child make and keep friends!

Chapter 1
What Are Social Skills?

S imply put, **social skills** are learned behaviors that children need in order to get along well with others in a majority of social situations. These skills include how children think about friendships and ways they act in a variety of social situations, such as at birthday parties, in restaurants, or on the playground. Social skills are what we use to "get by" in life. The ability to "get by" depends more on how well we get along with others than on how well we read, do math, or spell. Sometimes called "people skills," social skills are needed to have friendly interactions with others. They are what we use for making friends, having conversations, playing games, solving problems, and interviewing for jobs. Children learn some social skills naturally by seeing how others act and get along, but children also need help learning the social skills they lack.

Children who are having trouble making friends or keeping friendships going can learn how with a little help. Children need to learn what works (and what doesn't work) in different situations. They need to learn to be flexible, to "think on their feet," and to decide which behaviors are appropriate. This is no small task for anyone! It points to the importance of actively helping your child learn appropriate social skills.

Why Are Social Skills Important?

When you think about it, of all the skills that your child must learn in life, there are few as important as getting along with others. Whether in a classroom, at a bowling alley, in the supermarket, or applying for a job, your child's ability to make and keep friends is extremely important. If your child is able to make friends, play nicely, cooperate, and get along well with others, he/she will be more likely to enjoy positive experiences later in life. On the other hand, if your child argues and fights constantly, bullies others, or cannot carry on a conversation, he/she will likely continue to struggle through adulthood. In fact, research has shown that children who lack social skills are more likely to have serious problems later in life. They are more likely to drop out of school, lose jobs, have trouble with the police, and spend time in jail than children who have strong "people skills."

When children know that they are liked by others they feel proud, worthwhile, and good about themselves. They also gain a better sense of where they fit in a group and are able to find support among friends. Friends can reinforce your child's talents and help him/her to learn new skills. Children learn many positive things from their friends, and parents can actively help their children by talking about friendships and supervising playtime whenever possible. This sets the stage for good friendships.

Common Social Problems

One common complaint of parents is that their children do not seem to have friends. You may have heard your child ask, "Why don't they like me?" There are several differences between children who have friends and those who do not. Children who have many friends tend to share, say nice things, offer help, ask others to play, cooperate, and suggest compromises. Children who do not have many friends are rarely seen doing these things (Doll, Sheridan, & Law, 1989).

There are two basic types of behavior that affect a child's ability to make friends. First, there are children who tend to be shy or withdrawn. They don't play much with other children. Second, there are children who tend to use aggressive behaviors. They interact with other children, but do so in negative ways (they often argue and fight). Even though these behaviors are quite different from each other, both can cause problems in friendships.

Withdrawn Behavior

Children are exhibiting withdrawn behavior when they choose not to play much with other children and do not reach out to others. Instead, they stay by themselves in the classroom, on the playground, or at the park. They may watch others playing a game, but rarely ask if they can join in. They do not talk much. When they do, they usually use short answers to someone else's questions. They are often forgotten about by other children and are left out of games. Because of this, they miss chances to learn better ways of playing with others and solving problems. Since they don't learn important social skills from others (how can they learn from other children if they are not playing with them?), the differences between them and other children become greater as time goes on. This sometimes leads to other children teasing them or being left out of social events like parties or sports. It can also lead to feelings of sadness and loneliness that can continue throughout life.

Some children who demonstrate withdrawn behaviors also describe feelings of nervousness and anxiety when they interact with others. They complain of headaches or stomachaches when they are put on the spot, and usually do not know how to begin conversations appropriately or solve problems effectively. Rather, they stand quietly alone waiting for someone else to approach them. When they are in a problem situation, they often become victimized, ridiculed, teased, blamed, bullied, or taken advantage of in other ways. They generally lack assertiveness and do not stand up for themselves very effectively.

Example

Brittany is a shy, quiet fourth-grader. On the playground she is usually observed standing or swinging by herself. When Brittany is with other children, she is seen standing on the edge of a game or in the vicinity of a group, but not really interacting with the others. She is not usually selected to be on a team until all the other children are chosen. When it is her turn to play, Brittany wrings her hands nervously and whispers to herself "I can't do this!" If she makes a mistake and others yell at her or tease her, she stands sadly and quietly, not saying a word in her own defense. She is therefore seen as an "easy target" for the brunt of many jokes. If Brittany were able to learn and use some appropriate coping skills (e.g., problem-solving or dealing with teasing), she might be in a better position to stick up for herself or avoid such situations altogether.

Aggressive Behavior

Another common complaint of parents is that their children get into fights, arguments, and other conflicts frequently.

Example

When Chip has a problem with a classmate, brother, or sister, he begins raising his voice, arguing, and sometimes shoves or hits. Chip, the bully of his classroom, doesn't have the social skills to solve problems and get along with others. In situations that others might not consider problematic, Chip tries to get his way at all costs. He is simply not much fun to be around. Over time, he is excluded from games, parties, and other meaningful social activities.

The problems some children have with aggression are based partly on their difficulties using self-control and following rules. Their behavior is often described as impulsive. In many situations, children respond immediately and often seem "out of control." Because of this, they also have difficulty playing games and following rules. For example, children don't always play fairly. To children who aren't playing fairly, winning the game is more important than having fun or keeping a friend. So, they don't usually consider the rights of other children when playing. Children who play fairly, on the other hand, often say that keeping their friends is more important than winning the game.

Children who act aggressively also need help solving problems. Deciding if they have a problem and owning up to a problem are often difficult tasks for children who act aggressively. They also often overreact and have a hard time describing how to go about solving a problem.

Example

During an argument about who should be the first in line, Janice may not be able to state that there is a problem. When asked to think about possible solutions, she may give only one or two answers. Her answers will most likely be selfish ("I should go first no matter what!") or mean (shoving other children out of the way). She may have a hard time coming up with any positive or cooperative solutions. Asking Janice why she shoved the other students often leads to a dead-end response. It is likely that she doesn't know of any other possible actions. Even when Janice knows that there is a better, more appropriate solution, her impulsiveness often gets in the way. She tends to blame another or claim ignorance for a problem, using statements such as "She started it!" or "It's not my fault!"

Example

Another example is Stan. Stan wants to play Nintendo,™ but Phillip wants to play cards. Rather than thinking about different ways to solve the problem, such as compromising by playing cards first and Nintendo™ second, Stan argues and fights with Phillip until Phillip storms out of the house and goes home, screaming, "I'm never going to play with you again!" Stan is left alone, blaming Phillip for leaving as though he had nothing to do with it. When Stan's mother asks what happened, Stan responds with something like "Phillip is such a baby. I don't want to play with him anyway!"

Another problem often encountered by children who exhibit aggressive behavior is that they don't think about what will happen after they act a certain way. Many children who rely on aggressive actions to get what they want don't realize that there are many positive actions that work better. The first solution they think of is usually aggressive, and this is what they use. They tend to act first and think second (if at all), and never consider that their behavior has consequences. When they do think about consequences, they tend to be short-term ("I hit him and now I feel better") and not long-term ("even though I feel better now, I might get into big trouble with my parents and not be invited to play again"). A common consequence of these aggressive actions is that others begin rejecting the child. They are no longer included in activities and events, and miss out on opportunities to learn better ways of responding.

Children who don't have many friends not only behave differently than those who have many friends. They also think about situations, especially problems, differently. A common complaint of parents is that their children blame others for problems or fail to take responsibility for their actions. How many times have you heard your child say, "It wasn't my fault" or "I couldn't help it"? Often children don't realize that others have different opinions than they do. They typically don't think about others' feelings because they don't realize that someone else might feel differently. A child without friends may not know how to respond if you ask, "How would you feel if you were teased that way?" or "What do you think Sue was thinking when you said that to her?"

A lot of communication happens without words. Facial expressions, gestures, and other body language play important roles in communication. Also, the *way* children say things to each other is often more important than *what* they say. Children who don't play much with others don't always understand body language. Sometimes they believe that when something bad happens to them, it is because other children wanted it, even made it, happen. They believe that everyone dislikes them and is "out to get them."

Some children do not see the effect their behavior has on others. Partly because they don't read body language very well, these children don't see that others may not think it's "cool" to bully others in the playground or be disruptive in the classroom.

Example

Jack tries to stop a game of kickball by grabbing the ball and throwing it over the fence. He thinks this is a good way of getting attention and doesn't realize that the other children are irritated by his behavior. When no one selects Jack to be on their kickball team the next day, he screams, "It's not fair that you won't let me play! I'll show you!" He doesn't understand that his own actions caused him to be left out.

The Role of Parents

Parents play a very important role in their children's friendships. In many ways, parents set the stage for friendships by choosing certain neighborhoods and schools, arranging social events and outings, and providing examples of good (and sometimes questionable) social skills. By making a point of helping their children develop positive social relationships, parents are giving their children a head start.

There are many things you can do to help your child with friendships. But it takes work! You've probably heard the saying "Do what I say, not as I do." This doesn't work well with children. If you want your child to be kind and considerate, to share with others, to say nice things, and treat others nicely, then use these behaviors yourself. You can also help your child recognize others' feelings by discussing feelings and giving lots of support for talking about them.

Some children need help to learn how to get along with others. Some of the basic social skills covered in this book are: how to start friendships and interactions, how to keep a conversation going, how to play cooperatively, how to solve problems, how to make good decisions, and how to compromise. You can teach these skills by reviewing the steps in this book, showing how they can be used, having your child practice, and giving your child feedback.

By being there to help when your child is having problems with friends and talking to your child, you are helping him/her decide on positive solutions and reinforcing the use of positive social skills.

Helping your child develop better social skills is no small task. But read on—these are precisely the things you will be learning in this book.

Chapter 2
Which Social Skills Should I Focus On?

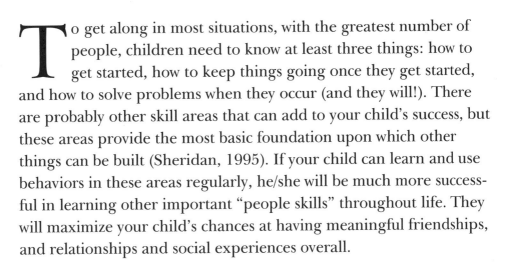

To get along in most situations, with the greatest number of people, children need to know at least three things: how to get started, how to keep things going once they get started, and how to solve problems when they occur (and they will!). There are probably other skill areas that can add to your child's success, but these areas provide the most basic foundation upon which other things can be built (Sheridan, 1995). If your child can learn and use behaviors in these areas regularly, he/she will be much more successful in learning other important "people skills" throughout life. They will maximize your child's chances at having meaningful friendships, and relationships and social experiences overall.

1. **How to get started:** There are four social entry skills that will help your child get started "on the right foot." They are: Body Basics, starting conversations, joining in, and noticing and talking about feelings. Each of these skills is composed of steps that your child can learn and remember.

2. **How to keep it going:** Skills in this domain are concerned with continuing positive experiences with others once the door has been opened. It is not enough to simply know how to start friendships; it is also important that children know how to maintain them. The two skills for Keeping It Going are: having conversations and playing cooperatively.

3. **How to solve problems**: Problems emerge in all human relationships and interactions. Children's friendships are no exception. Learning many appropriate social skills provides an opportunity for your child to avoid problems, but keep in mind that some problems will still occur. Even if your child's problems do not seem very important to you, they are very important to your child! Your child can learn a lot from the problems he/she encounters, and teaching your child how to solve his/her own problems is an important life skill. Your child will use problem-solving (and all the other skills covered in this book) throughout life.

In this chapter, skills in each of these three areas will be detailed and examples provided. Use Box 2-1 as an easy reference of these sets of social skills.

As you read about each skill, refer to the corresponding Social Skills Card at the back of the book. Each card provides: a review of the skill steps, important reminders about using the skill, and

---

BOX 2-1

Social Skills for Getting Started, Keeping It Going, and Solving Problems

Getting Started
1. Body Basics (FEVER)
2. Starting a Conversation
3. Joining In
4. Noticing and Talking About Feelings

Keeping It Going
1. Having a Conversation
2. Playing Cooperatively

Solving Problems
1. Solving Problems
2. Controlling Anger
3. Solving Arguments
4. Dealing With Teasing
5. Dealing With Being Left Out
6. Accepting "No"

ideas for coaching, modeling, and practicing the skill with your child. (A discussion of techniques for coaching, modeling, and practicing the skills is in Chapter 3.) Examples are provided in this chapter for your convenience. Referring to the cards as you go along will help you be more comfortable with the material when you start working with your child.

Getting Started

In order for your child to make new friends, he/she will have to learn how to get started. Some ways of gaining attention or joining a game work better than others. Waiting for the right time and asking calmly is better than shouting "Hey, I want a turn!" Likewise, using a friend's name and asking a question is better than poking or shoving.

Example

When Liz sees a classmate that she wants to talk to, she runs over, pulls her arm, and blurts out, "Hey!" When she does this, Liz often receives very negative reactions. The other children usually respond to her by saying "Knock it off!" or "Get out of here!"

When Chaia wants to get into a game of soccer, she stands by the sidelines and watches, never saying a word but hoping that someone will notice her. Chaia is usually ignored.

These approaches don't work well, and neither Liz nor Chaia get to play further because they did not start correctly. Getting things started in the right way is one key to making friends. The Getting Started skills will help your child get off on the right foot with friends.

Body Basics

Body Basics (Jones, Sheridan, & Binns, 1993) are some general things we all do with our faces and bodies that communicate a lot to others, even when few words are spoken. They include things like facial gestures (such as smiles, frowns, or pouts), tone of voice (such as whining or using a snippy voice), and posture (such as standing with hands on hips, fists clenched, or head and shoulders slumped over).

Much of what we communicate to others is communicated through our body language rather than our words. When you use a stern tone of voice, you are communicating to another person that you are very serious about what you are saying. When you look away rather than directly at another person, you may be communicating that you do not feel comfortable about what is being said or done. When you point at another person or clench your fists, you could be communicating anger toward the person. When you tap your toes or fingers and look continuously at your watch, you may be telling others that you are impatient. Children need to learn how body language contributes to a message. They can learn how their own body language conveys messages and how to "read" the body language of others.

Many children don't realize that the way they look at others and how they say things are as important as what they say. Good Body Basics are things that children can do each time they talk or play with other children to set up a good interaction.

Good Body Basics can be remembered by using the word "FEVER." Each letter of FEVER stands for one of the Body Basics. These basic skills convey to others that you care about what is being said and done, that you are listening and paying attention, and that you are comfortable with the other person. They should be taught first because they can be used with every skill, in every social situation. One way that you might convey the importance of these skills is to demonstrate "good" and "bad" Body Basics and have your child tell you what he/she saw. (For example, you might look at the floor rather than in their eyes when talking.) You might also have your child look into a mirror and have a conversation with himself/herself, and then ask your child to comment on his/her own Body Basics. Using a tape recorder to tape a conversation with your child also provides a good opportunity to discuss voice tone.

FACE the other person: When talking or playing with others, it is a good idea to face them. Many children turn their backs to others or try speaking before they have the attention of the other person. By facing a person when talking, the other person is more likely to pay attention, listen to what is being said, and respond favorably.

Use EYE contact: It is important that children learn to look people in the eyes when talking. This conveys interest in the other person and helps stress the importance of what is being said. Using eye contact is not the same as staring uncomfortably or inappropriately. Rather, it requires a comfortable, friendly gaze into another's eyes and face.

Use the right VOICE: Help your child understand that what he/she says is not always as important as how it is said. Speaking in a voice that others can hear, that is not raised, and that is calm and smooth helps others focus on what is being said. Help your child recognize various tones of voice by using many examples. Children often don't know how they sound to other people.

Watch EXPRESSIONS: A helpful skill for children to learn is the ability to notice their own expressions, and the expressions of others. Sometimes a child feels one way but his/her facial expression suggests something very different. What is being said is then misinterpreted by others.

Example

Fran doesn't get many invitations to Romanita's house because when asked, Fran looks down at her feet and shrugs her shoulders. Even though Fran doesn't mean to look sad, that is how other children read her expression. If Fran were actually happy about being invited, it would be best to smile, nod, use eye contact with Romanita, and say something like "sure!" when asked to play.

Many times children don't understand what other people are "saying" with their faces. Helping your own child learn to read facial expressions will help him/her to notice and adjust his/her own expressions.

Example

Jorge often laughs when other children make mistakes in the classroom. Because he doesn't realize that the looks he is getting from his classmates are angry, he doesn't understand why no one picks him to work with on a class project. If Jorge were able to read the expressions of the other children, he would interpret their looks as indicating their displeasure with his laughing. He might begin to understand that others do not like his behaviors, and he might stop his laughing in order to get along better with his classmates.

Use the RIGHT body posture and Relax: Using the right body posture and relaxing means standing or sitting comfortably and attentively when with others (rather than being stiff or slouching). When children slouch they appear disinterested in playing with others. When children put their hands on their hips, fold their arms, clench their fists, or tense their jaws and foreheads they appear angry. Many times children don't realize that they are doing these things. Helping your child recognize body language will assist him/her in becoming aware of his/her own feelings.

Example

When Rebecca starts getting angry, she usually tenses up her forehead and mouth. Once this happens, her mother anticipates Rebecca's pouting and screaming, saying things like "That's not fair!" If Rebecca learned to recognize her own body signs, she might be able to deal with her anger as soon as she realizes that she is tensing up.

As you review this section on Body Basics with your child, refer to Box 2-2 and Social Skills Card 1 for Do's and Don'ts that will help you illustrate FEVER for your child. Steps for modeling and practicing are also included at the end of the section and on the back of Social Skills Card 1. Coaching, modeling, and practicing are discussed in detail in Chapters 3 and 4.

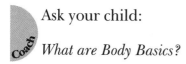

Ask your child:

What are Body Basics?

▸ Actions or behaviors we use that send messages to others, sometimes without even using words.

BOX 2-2

GETTING STARTED: BODY BASICS

STEPS OF FEVER:

1. **FACE** the other person.
2. Use **EYE** contact.
3. Use an appropriate **VOICE**.
4. Watch **EXPRESSIONS**.
5. Use the **RIGHT** posture and Relax.

DO:

▸ Remember FEVER.
▸ Smile.
▸ Count to 5 or 10 if you need to relax.
▸ Use friendly words.
▸ Take a deep breath before talking.
▸ Stay in your own space.

DON'T:

▸ Stare at the other person.
▸ Look at your feet or somewhere else.
▸ Get too close or be too far away.
▸ Mumble your words or slouch.
▸ Clench your fists or jaw.

▸ Things we do with our face and bodies while we are talking to or playing with others.

▸ Important body signs that can be remembered with the word FEVER: Face the other person, use Eye contact, use the right Voice, watch Expressions, use the Right body posture and Relax.

Ask your child:

Why is it important to use good Body Basics? In what situations would you use this skill?

▸ To let others know you like them or are interested in what they are saying or doing

▸ To help yourself feel confident when interacting with or talking to others

Say to your child:

Let's pretend that I want to ask my teacher for permission to get a book from my locker. This is what I would do. Watch closely and tell me which Body Basics I use and which I forget.

- Show your child FEVER by remembering all of the steps or forgetting some. (For a discussion of modeling see Chapter 3.)

- Ask your child what you did well and what you could do better.

- Ask for feedback about the specific steps of FEVER.

Say to your child:

Practice

Now pretend that you want to ask your teacher for some help with a math problem. Go through the steps of Body Basics (FEVER).

- Practice FEVER with your child, watching what he/she does to use the steps. (For a description of practicing, see Chapter 3.)

- Tell your child what he/she did well and what to work on.

- Have your child practice again, until all the skill steps are followed correctly.

- Ask your child when this skill can be used at school or other places.

Starting a Conversation

Starting a conversation is the first step toward making a friend. It often opens the door to learning about others, their likes and dislikes, common interests, and other important aspects of friendship-making. When your child sees someone he/she would like to play with or talk to, encourage him/her to start a conversation. Sometimes children stand back and don't do anything to

start a conversation. Other times children shout "Hey" or interrupt games or conversations. More appropriate ways to start a
conversation are to use the other person's name, ask a question,
give a compliment, or relate an interesting story.

Steps for starting a conversation and Do's and Don'ts that you can
review with your child are listed in Box 2-3 and on Social Skills
Card 2.

Ask your child:

What does it mean to start a conversation?

> ‣ To begin talking to someone who you aren't
> already talking to.

> ‣ To start talking about something you want to talk
> about.

> ‣ To ask questions if you need an answer.

Ask your child:

*Why is it important to know how to start a conversation? In
what situations would you use this skill?*

> ‣ You might want to play with or talk to the person.

> ‣ You might need to have a question answered.

List the skill steps and ask your child to repeat them.

Say to your child:

*Let's pretend that I want to tell my friend about a new puppy
that I got. This is what I would do. Watch closely and tell me
which steps I use and which steps I forget.*

- Demonstrate the steps of starting a conversation by remembering all of the steps or forgetting some. (For a discussion of modeling, see Chapter 3.)

- Ask your child what you did well and what you could do better.

- Ask for feedback about the specific steps of starting a conversation.

Practice

Say to your child:

Now pretend that you want to tell your friend about a movie you went to. Go through the steps of starting a conversation.

- Practice starting a conversation with your child, watching what he/she does to follow the steps. (For a discussion of practicing, see Chapter 3.)

- Tell your child what was done well and what to work on.

BOX 2-3

GETTING STARTED: STARTING A CONVERSATION

STEPS:

1. Use Body Basics (FEVER).

2. Greet the other person (say "hi" and use their name).

3. Decide what to say (ask a question, give a compliment, or talk about something in common.)

4. Wait for the right time.

5. Start talking (in a calm and friendly tone of voice).

DO:

- Remember FEVER.
- Smile.
- Take a deep breath before talking.
- Use friendly words.

DON'T:

- Yell or whisper.
- Interrupt the other person if he/she is talking or working.
- Use inappropriate words.
- Get into the other person's space.

- Have your child practice until all the skill steps are followed correctly.

- Ask your child when this skill can be used at school or other places.

Joining In

Joining a game or activity that is already in progress is sometimes hard. By learning how to join in, your child is making a positive step toward making friends and getting along. He/she will be able to play with others who are already playing, have fun with a group, and become part of a group. Follow the steps in Box 2-4 or on Social Skills Card 3.

Example

When Nico grabs the basketball during the game so that he can be included, he is not setting the stage for making friends. Neither is Yolanda creating friendship possibilities when she watches a group of girls eat lunch together while she eats alone.

It would be better for Nico to approach the children playing basketball, wait for a time out in the game, call the names of one or two players, and ask "Can I join the game?" Yolanda, on the other hand, could walk up to the table of girls, wait for a break in their conversation, look them in the eyes, and say "Is it OK if I sit here and eat lunch with you?"

Ask your child:

What does it mean to join in?

> ‣ To play with others who are already playing a game.

> ‣ To do something with a group of other children.

Ask your child:

Why is it important to know how to join in? In what situations would you use this skill?

> ‣ To be able to play with others.

> ‣ To have fun with a group of children.

> ‣ To become part of a group.

BOX 2-4

GETTING STARTED: JOINING IN

STEPS:

1. Use Body Basics (FEVER).

2. Greet the other person.

3. Wait for the right time.

4. Ask to join ("Can I join you?" or "Can I play too?").

DO:

> ‣ Remember the Body Basics.
> ‣ Smile.
> ‣ Use friendly words.

DON'T:

> ‣ Yell or whisper.
> ‣ Interrupt the other person.
> ‣ Use inappropriate words.
> ‣ Get too close or too far from the other

List the skill steps and ask your child to repeat them.

Say to your child:

Let's pretend that I want to walk home from school with two girls who live in the neighborhood. This is what I would do. Watch closely and tell me which steps I use and which steps I forget.

> ‣ Show your child the steps of joining in by remembering all the steps or forgetting some. (For a discussion of modeling, see Chapter 3.)

- Ask your child what you did well and what you could do better.

- Ask about the skill steps and Body Basics.

Practice

Say to your child:

Now pretend that you see me and another child eating lunch together and you want to eat with us. Go through the steps of joining in.

- Practice joining in with your child, watching what he/she does to follow the steps. (For a description of practicing, see Chapter 3.)

- Tell your child what was done well and what to work on.

- Have your child practice until all the skill steps are followed correctly.

- Ask your child when this skill can be used at school or other places.

Noticing and Talking About Feelings

Noticing and talking about feelings strengthens your child's ability to understand his/her own emotions and the emotions of others, and helps your child to express this understanding when it is important. It is a difficult skill for many individuals (including many adults), so don't be surprised if it isn't easy for your child. Young or inexperienced children may not use "feeling words" very effectively. When asked how he felt during an argument, for example, seven-year-old Zach responded "I felt like I just wanted to hit him!" Zach doesn't realize that his comment reflected behaviors, not feelings. If he were able to understand his emotions better, Zach might have responded that he felt frustrated, misunderstood, or impatient.

Young children like Zach often have difficulties pinpointing their feelings. Even when they use "feeling words," they tend to be basic ones like "mad," "sad," "happy," or "glad." More complex emotions enter a child's vocabulary a little later, and by the age of nine or ten, a child might be able to use words like "annoyed," "anxious," or "frightened." Children who have difficulties with friends often express their feelings by using the word "mad." For example, when children tease or bully Nick on the playground, he reports feeling "really mad." Anger and madness are typically second feelings that "cover up" the true feelings underneath. With prompting (reminding that "mad" is a second feeling), Nick comes to realize that he was really feeling embarrassed.

One way to help children notice how they feel is to ask them to pay attention to "body cues," or "body signs." These are physical changes the body goes through when emotions kick in. For example, some children report that they feel their face turn red or their forehead and eyes tense up when they become uncomfortable. Others say that they feel "butterflies" in their stomachs or their heart beat faster when they are nervous or uptight. Body cues are important. If your child can pick out body cues that indicate certain emotions, he/she will be in a better position to handle those emotions.

Noticing and expressing their own feelings and recognizing how others feel are skills that children can use every day.

Expressing Feelings: Helping children to notice and talk about their feelings helps them to get along with others. When children are able to express their feelings they are better able to:

- Make friends because they are relating on a personal/feeling level: "I feel calm when we sing together. How do you feel?"

- Ask for what they want and so are more likely to receive it: "I feel left out because everyone else got a cookie but I didn't."

- Draw boundaries with others: "Cassie, I don't like when you use my blocks without asking," says Linda. Next time, when Cassie asks first, Linda and Cassie play together.

- Relate to others their appreciation and so have pleasurable experiences repeated:

  "I felt happy when we saw the seals playing at the zoo with your Uncle Bill," says Daniel.

  Cele replies, "Uncle Bill is taking me to the museum next week. Do you want to come too?"

- Elicit compassion and support from others:

  When Pablo says, "I feel so nervous about going to the new class that I have butterflies in my stomach," Emilio responds by saying, "I can show you where your seat is."

Unexpressed feelings get stored up inside, causing hurt, anger, depression, anxiety, and poor self-image. Children often lash out at others when they feel sad, upset, frustrated, embarrassed, humiliated, or left out. Angry outbursts and overreacting are often the result of not expressing underlying feelings.

Recognizing How Others Feel: Noticing how others feel is just as important in your child's friendships as expressing his/her own feelings. It shows others that your child cares about them. When your child learns to recognize the emotions behind body language such as clenched fists, downcast eyes, and glares, he/she can respond in a positive manner.

Other body cues that your child might notice in others include: smiles, folded arms, scowls, and hands on hips. Box 2-5 lists several body cues, and suggestions of feelings that might be conveyed. You might find it helpful to go over these with your child (either list them or demonstrate them for your child) and ask your child what feelings could be underneath each body sign.

BOX 2-5

WHAT BODY CUES CONVEY

Body Cues ▶	Feelings
Smiling ▶	Happiness
Frowning ▶	Sadness
Scowling ▶	Anger
Arms folded ▶	Impatience, anger
Pointing ▶	Seriousness
Crying ▶	Sadness
Voice shaking ▶	Sadness, nervousness
Hands on hips ▶	Anger, disappointment
Gasping ▶	Surprise, disbelief
Yawning ▶	Boredom
Jumping ▶	Excitement
Shaking, trembling ▶	Fear

Ben and Franco are working together on a class project. Franco works slowly and carefully, but Ben is in a hurry to finish so he can be the first one outside for recess. Franco wants to do the work accurately and is not interested in being the first one done. Each time Ben says "Hurry up!" or "That's good enough. Let's move on," Franco becomes irritated and scowls at Ben, slowing their work even more.

Ben is in too much of a hurry to notice Franco's body language and continues pestering Franco. Pretty soon Franco loses his patience and blurts out, "Quit bugging me! I'm doing the best I can to get it right!" Upon hearing the outburst, their teacher requires both boys to stay in for recess. If Ben had done a better job at recognizing Franco's facial expression, he might have realized that Franco was working hard and becoming very frustrated, impatient, and losing his ability to remain calm. Ben could have said to Franco, "I know this is important to you. What can I do to help get it done correctly and quickly?"

Refer to the steps for noticing and talking about feelings in Box 2-6 and Social Skills Card 4 when helping your child. As he/she is learning, use the Do's and Don'ts as reminders.

Say to your child:

What does it mean to notice and express feelings?

> ▶ To be able to tell how you are feeling, or how someone else might be feeling.

- To be able to talk about how you are feeling using feeling words.

- To understand body cues (such as clenched fists or jaw, upset stomach, glaring eyes, slumped posture), facial cues (such as smiles, frowns, tears), and voice tone (such as whispering, yelling).

Ask your child:

Why is it important to notice how you feel or how others feel? In what situations would you use this skill?

- It can help us understand ourselves/the other person.

- To show the other person that we care about them.

- So that others know how we feel.

- To let others understand our feelings and treat us nicer.

- So our feelings don't get stored up inside and cause us to hurt inside.

- So our feelings don't come out in a way that we don't want.

List the skill steps and ask your child to repeat them.

Say to your child:

Let's pretend that I want to tell my friend that I was disappointed when I wasn't invited to her party. This is what I would do. Watch closely and tell me which steps I use and which steps I forget.

- Demonstrate noticing and talking about feelings by remembering all of the steps or forgetting some.

- Ask your child what you did well and what you could do better.

- Ask for feedback about the specific steps of noticing and talking about feelings.

Say to your child:

Now pretend that you want to tell your friend that you were hurt when your classmates were joking about your new haircut. Go through the steps.

- Practice noticing and talking about feelings with your child by having your child use the steps. (For a description of practicing, see Chapter 3.)

- Tell your child what he/she did well and what to work on.

- Have your child practice until all the skill steps are followed correctly.

- Ask your child when this skill can be used at school or other places.

Keeping It Going

Getting things started is the first move toward making friends. Beyond that, your child needs to know how to keep a friendly interaction going. The skills for Keeping It Going are: having a conversation, and playing cooperatively. As with the skill sets for Getting Started, each is composed of steps that your child can learn. Chapters 3 and 4 provide techniques for teaching your child the skill steps and helping him/her to put them into practice. Use the Social Skills Cards in the back of the book as an easy reference when teaching your child the skills.

Having a Conversation

Conversations are an important part of making friends. When children converse they learn new things, find out information, share ideas, and find out what they have in common with others. When your child learns to start and keep a conversation going, he/she will soon connect with other children who have the same favorite sports team, like the same TV shows, or live in the same neighborhood. Having common interests is one of the first things children pick up on when making friends. The steps of having a conversation are listed in Box 2-7 and on Social Skills Card 5 along with some Do's and Don'ts. An important part of conversation is having a topic in mind and sticking to it. Beyond asking a question or making a statement about that topic, your child can learn to say or ask at least two or three more things related to the topic. This allows your

BOX 2-7

KEEPING IT GOING: HAVING A CONVERSATION

STEPS:

1. Use Body Basics (FEVER).

2. Wait your turn (don't interrupt or blurt out).

3. Say what you want to say, or ask your question.

4. Listen to the other person.

5. Say or ask at least two more things during the conversation.

6. Make a closing remark (e.g., "See you later," "Hope it works out," or "Good-bye").

DO:

- ▶ Remember the Body Basics.
- ▶ Smile.
- ▶ Use friendly words.

DON'T:

- ▶ Yell or whisper.
- ▶ Interrupt the other person.
- ▶ Use inappropriate words.

child to find out the other person's opinion, experiences, or ideas. It also allows your child to share what is important to him/her.

Listening is often the key to having a satisfying conversation. Many children (and adults) talk without letting anyone else say a word. Others allow people to talk, but insist that the others are wrong. Being open-minded in a conversation is important because it invites discussion on a certain topic without escalating the conversation to an argument. Good listening skills include the Body Basics. Beyond that, a good listener often repeats back what he/she hears, nods, or says "mm hmm," and makes sure he/she understands what the other person is saying.

Example

When other children ask her questions, Jessie looks at her feet and shrugs her shoulders. She doesn't answer their questions or add her own opinions or ideas. For example, when Cara asked her if she liked the school play, she simply nodded her head and said "yeah." To carry on a conversation, Jessie might have looked into Cara's eyes and responded by saying "Yes, I thought it was great! What did you think?"

Ask your child:

What does it mean to have a conversation?

> ▸ To spend time with a person talking.

> ▸ To talk about school, movies, sports, or something you both like or that you have in common, etc.

Ask your child:

Why is it important to know how to have a conversation? In what situations would you use this skill?

> ▸ To be able to talk to others.

> ▸ To tell others something important.

> ▸ To find out something from others.

List the skill steps and ask your child to repeat them.

Say to your child:

Let's pretend that I want to tell my brother about what I did in school today. This is what I would do. Watch closely and tell me which steps I use and which steps I forget.

> ▸ Show your child the steps of having a conversation by remembering all of the steps or forgetting some. (For a discussion of modeling, see Chapter 3.)

> ▸ Ask your child what you did well and what you could do better.

- Ask for feedback about the specific steps of having a conversation.

Say to your child:

Now pretend that you want to tell your friend about a new toy you got. Go through the steps of having a conversation.

- Practice having a conversation with your child, watching what he/she does to follow the steps. (For a description of practicing, see Chapter 3.)

- Tell your child what was done well and what to work on.

- Have your child practice until all the skill steps are followed correctly.

- Ask your child when this skill can be used at school or other places.

Playing Cooperatively

Another component of Keeping It Going is playing cooperatively. Many parents worry when their child does not play with others in a cooperative, friendly way. Arguing about the rules of a game, not sharing toys, boasting about being the best, and putting other children down are common problems. An important social skill for all play situations is cooperating. Cooperating means playing or working together in a fair way. It includes sharing, taking turns, following rules, helping each other, and compromising.

When children cooperate, they tend to get along because everyone knows what to do. Playing fairly and cooperating simply make games more fun.

You have probably witnessed children playing who weren't cooperating. A lot of time is spent arguing or fighting, which gets in the way of playing for fun and friendship.

Use the steps in Box 2-8 and Social Skills Card 6 with your child to teach him/her how to play cooperatively. Also discuss sharing, helping others, taking turns, and following rules.

Ask your child:

What does it mean to play co-operatively?

- To play together in a fair way.

- To share, take turns, and help each other.

Ask your child:

Why is it important to know how to play cooperatively? In what situations would you use this skill?

- So everyone knows what to do.

- To be able to get along when playing.

- To make the game more fun.

BOX 2-8

KEEPING IT GOING: PLAYING COOPERATIVELY

STEPS:

1. Use Body Basics (FEVER).

2. Decide who starts (read the directions, flip a coin, roll a die).

3. Wait your turn.

4. Talk and listen to the other person (have a conversation).

5. Say something nice at the end (e.g., "good game," "that was fun," or "thanks for playing").

DO:

- Smile.
- Use friendly words.
- Look at the directions if you don't know them.

DON'T:

- Yell, whisper, or use inappropriate words.
- Argue about the rules of the game.
- Be a sore loser.

List the skill steps and ask your child to repeat them.

Say to your child:

Model

Let's pretend that I am playing a game of cards with my friend. This is what I would do. Watch closely and tell me which steps I use and which steps I forget.

> ‣ Show your child the steps of playing cooperatively by remembering all of the steps or forgetting some. (For a discussion of modeling, see Chapter 3.)

> ‣ Ask your child what you did well and what you could do better.

> ‣ Ask for feedback about the specific steps of playing cooperatively.

Say to your child:

Practice

Now pretend that you are playing checkers with your friend. Go through the steps of playing cooperatively.

> ‣ Practice playing cooperatively with your child, watching what he/she does to follow the steps. (For a description of practicing, see Chapter 3.)

> ‣ Tell your child what was done well and what to work on.

> ‣ Have your child practice until all the skill steps are followed correctly.

> ‣ Ask your child when this skill can be used at school or other places.

Solving Problems

Even if your child learns all of the skills for Getting Started and keeping things going, chances are that he/she will still encounter problems with friends from time to time. The specific problems will change from one situation to the next, but the steps for solving problems are similar in each case. The strategies that will be addressed in this section are: controlling anger, solving arguments, dealing with teasing, handling being left out, and accepting "no" for an answer. All of the problems use the same five steps, even though the solutions may change. Using the same five steps for all problem situations will make it easier for your child to learn and remember this important skill. He/she can then apply the steps to a variety of situations.

Chapter 3 outlines what you can do to teach your child skills to solve problems. When teaching your child, use the corresponding Social Skills Cards in the back of the book.

Problem-Solving Skills

Children learn a lot about life from the problems they experience. Helping them solve the problems they face today will prepare them to solve problems in the future.

There are five basic steps to solving problems. These steps can be used in any kind of situation, and not only those that are described in this section. As with the other social skills, Body Basics are essential. Suggestions for what to do and what not to do when solving problems are in Box 2-9 and on Social Skills Card 7. Once your child learns these steps well, he/she will be able to engage and complete them pretty quickly. These five steps of

BOX 2-9

SOLVING PROBLEMS

STEPS:

1. Stop, take a deep breath, and count to five.

2. Decide what the problem is and how you feel.

3. Think about your choices and their consequences.

4. Decide on your best choice.

5. Do it.

DO:

- Remember the Body Basics.
- Relax.
- Tell yourself to be calm.
- Think of at least three choices.
- Use "I" statements.

DON'T:

- Yell, scream, or use inappropriate words.
- Call the other person names.
- Hit or kick the other person.
- Use "they" statements.

problem-solving can be used "on the spot" whenever conflicts arise:

1. **Stop, take a deep breath, and count to five.** This allows your child to relax so he/she can think clearly.

2. **Decide what the problem is and how you feel.** This step is sometimes hard for children, especially those who do not always admit that they have a problem. Help your child learn to "own" his/her problems and feelings. Direct your child to use "I" statements, such as "I have a problem…"; "My problem is…"; and "I feel…". These are better than "they" statements, which start out by describing what someone else did which your child cannot control. Your child can only control his/her own actions and feelings.

"I" statements also help children "own" their behaviors and feelings. Remember that certain "I"statements do not count, such as "I hate that." Refer to the examples of "they" statements and "I" statements in Box 2-10. Read some of them to your child to show what it means to use "I" statements. Then turn some of your child's "they" statements into "I" statements.

3. **Think about your choices and their consequences.** There is more than one way to handle just about any problem. Children need help thinking about all of their choices and

weighing the consequences of each possible solution. Encourage your child to come up with at least three positive choices to his/her problem, since the first one doesn't always work. Sometimes two or more choices are used in combination. Let your child do most of the thinking, but help him/her come up with some choices if necessary.

Part of discussing choices is thinking about consequences. Consequences are what happen as a result of acting on a choice. Consequences can be immediate (what might happen right away) or long-term (what might occur over time). Children don't normally think about the consequences of their actions, so talking about them is really important.

Tips for talking about choices and consequences with your child are provided in Chapter 4.

BOX 2-10

"THEY" STATEMENTS VS. "I" STATEMENTS

"THEY" STATEMENTS:
- Marissa didn't invite me to her party.
- They never let me play with them!
- Justin makes me so mad!
- Keevan was fighting with me.
- Stacey was being mean!
- No one likes me!
- They made me cry at lunchtime.
- No one picked me to be on their team.

"I" STATEMENTS:
- I wasn't invited to Marissa's party.
- I was left out of the game at recess.
- I was mad when Justin took my book.
- I was in a fight with Keevan.
- I felt hurt by what Stacey was doing.
- I feel left out.
- I cried when the other children took my lunch.
- I wanted to play but I wasn't chosen.

Example

Emily becomes quite upset when Jason teases her. She thinks about several choices, such as telling him how she feels, ignoring him, or walking away. She decides that expressing her feelings may actually provoke more teasing, so she decides to ignore him. When that doesn't work, she walks away and finds that stops the teasing.

4. **Decide on your best choice.** After your child thinks about his/her choices and their consequences, it's time to select the choice that is best. Let your child decide which choice is best, even though you may have your own favorite. (The importance of letting your child make his/her own choice is discussed further in Chapter 4.) By letting your child make decisions, you are fostering self-reliance. Your child will "own" the problem and the solution and will gradually learn to solve problems, even when you are not there to help.

   Of course, there are some cases when you cannot let your child follow through on a choice because it would harm him/her or someone else. In this case, you will have to step in and insist that they choose something else, explaining that some choices are unacceptable because they are dangerous or harmful.

5. **Do it.** After your child has followed all the steps and made a choice for solving the problem, the next step is to do it. When a situation arises that calls for problem-solving, encourage your child to use all of the steps. In fact, it's a good idea to help him/her anticipate specific times when he/she will need to use the steps by discussing common problems and when

they normally occur. Guidelines for talking about problems and setting goals with your child are discussed more thoroughly in Chapter 4.

After your child follows through with the choice, he/she should ask "How did I do?" If your child feels that the problem is not solved, he/she may need to try again using another choice.

Example

Felipe and Rocco both want a carton of chocolate milk with lunch, but there is only one left. Rocco insists that he get the chocolate milk, but Felipe really wants it also. They begin to argue. When Felipe notices his fists clench and his heart beat faster, he stops, takes a deep breath, and counts silently to five. He thinks to himself: "We both want the same milk, but there's only one. I could keep arguing, but that will turn into a bigger problem, we'll get in trouble, and we'll probably have to stay in for recess. If I suggest a compromise, maybe we'll both be happy and get some of what we each want." Felipe then says to Rocco: "We both want the chocolate milk, but there's only one left. How about if I get a glass and we split it? Then we could both have some." Rocco says "OK," and the boys end up having a great time eating lunch together.

Ask your child:

What does it mean to solve problems?

> ▸ To use steps to deal with problems when they occur.

- To know how to act or behave when there is a problem with others.

Ask your child:

Why is it important to solve problems? In what situations would you use this skill?

- To keep friends.

- To get along better with friends, parents, and others.

- To know how to deal with problems when they come up.

List the skill steps and ask your child to repeat them.

Say to your child:

Let's pretend that I am watching my favorite TV show and my sister comes into the room and changes the channel. This is what I would do. Watch closely and tell me which steps I use and which steps I forget.

- Demonstrate the steps of solving problems by remembering all of the steps or forgetting some. When demonstrating the steps of solving problems, indicate what you are thinking about the problem, choices, and consequences by whispering the thoughts. (For a discussion of modeling, see Chapter 3.)

- Ask your child what you did well and what you could do better.

> Ask for feedback about the specific steps of solving problems.

Practice

Say to your child:

Now pretend that you are reading a book and a friend takes it from you. Go through the steps of solving problems.

> Practice solving problems with your child, watching what he/she does to follow the steps. (For a description of practicing, see Chapter 3.)

> Tell your child what was done well and what to work on.

> Have your child practice until all skill steps are followed correctly.

> Ask your child when this skill can be used at school or other places.

Controlling Anger

All children get angry at times. In fact, when asked how they feel when something bad happens, "mad" is almost always their first answer. Some children are able to deal with feeling angry

---

BOX 2-11

SOLVING PROBLEMS: CONTROLLING ANGER

STEPS:

1. Stop, take a deep breath, and count to five.

2. Decide what the problem is and how you feel.

3. Think about your choices and their consequences. (Emphasize positive choices.)

4. Decide on your best choice.

5. Do it.

DO:

> Remember the Body Basics.
> Relax.
> Tell yourself to calm down and that it's OK.
> Talk calmly.
> Compromise.
> Think of at least three choices.

DON'T:

> Yell, scream, or use inappropriate words.
> Call the other person names.
> Hit or kick.

---

pretty well; others lose control. Children need help recognizing the signs that they are becoming angry. Recognizing the signs is the first step in exercising self-control.

Your child will get along better with others, feel better about himself/herself, and be better able to solve problems when controlling his/her anger.

Box 2-11 shows the steps for controlling anger (also refer to Social Skills Card 8). The steps used are the same as those for solving problems (Box 2-9), but some of the choices your child identifies may be different.

Positive choices for controlling anger include:

- Ignoring the situation.

- Telling yourself "It's OK."

- Telling yourself to relax.

- Talking calmly.

- Compromising.

- Saying how you feel by using an "I" statement (refer to Box 2-10 if you need help).

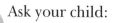 Ask your child:

What does it mean to use self control?

- To remain calm when you get angry, disappointed, frustrated, or when you don't get your way.

- To keep from getting into fights.

Why Don't They Like Me?

Ask your child:

Why is it important to use self-control? In what situations would you use this skill?

> ▸ To get along with others.

> ▸ To stay out of trouble.

> ▸ To feel better about yourself.

> ▸ To solve problems calmly and to keep friends.

List the skill steps and ask your child to repeat them.

Model Say to your child:

Let's pretend that my mom says I cannot watch a video because I did not clean my room. This is what I would do. Watch closely and tell me which steps I use and which steps I forget.

> ▸ Show your child the steps of controlling anger by remembering all of the steps or forgetting some. (For a discussion of modeling, see Chapter 3.)

> ▸ Ask your child what you did well and what you could do better.

> ▸ Ask for feedback about the specific steps of controlling anger.

Practice Say to your child:

Now pretend that you are at school and someone took your new soccer ball. Go through the steps of controlling your anger.

- Practice controlling anger with your child, watching what he/she does to follow the steps. (For a description of practicing, see Chapter 3.)

- Tell your child what was done well and what to work on.

- Have your child practice until all the skill steps are followed correctly.

- Ask your child when this skill can be used at school or other places.

Solving Arguments

One of the most common problems children have is getting into arguments with their friends and siblings. Some children do not realize that they can solve their problems calmly. Following the steps for solving arguments helps children learn that they have control over their own behavior, and that they can create positive outcomes.

There are five steps to solving arguments. As with other social difficulties, the Body Basics set the stage for solving the problem. The skill steps for solving arguments are described in Box 2-12 and on Social Skills Card 9. Reminders of what to do and what not to do are also included. For more information on each step, you may want to review the general steps for solving problems. When solving arguments, emphasize positive choices, such as:

- Compromising.

- Taking turns.

- Asking someone else for help.

- Saying how you feel by using "I" statements.

- Talking calmly.

- Telling yourself it's OK.

Ask your child:

What does it mean to solve arguments?

> - To stop an argument before it gets too bad.

> - To use self-control when in an argument.

Ask your child:

Why is it important to solve arguments? In what situations would you use this skill?

> - To get along better with others.

> - To keep friends.

List the skill steps and ask your child to repeat them.

Say to your child:

Let's pretend that my friend and I disagree about the rules of a new game. This is what I would do. Watch closely and tell me which steps I use and which steps I forget.

BOX 2-12

SOLVING PROBLEMS: ARGUMENTS

STEPS:

1. Stop, take a deep breath, and count to five.

2. Decide what the problem is and how you feel.

3. Think about your choices and their consequences.

4. Decide on your best choice.

5. Do it.

DO:

> - Remember the Body Basics.
> - Compromise.
> - Tell yourself to be calm and that it's OK.
> - Think of at least three positive choices to solve the argument.

DON'T:

> - Yell, scream, or use inappropriate words.
> - Call the other person names.
> - Hit, kick, or argue with the other person.

- Demonstrate solving arguments by remembering all of the steps or forgetting some. (For a discussion of modeling, see Chapter 3.)

- Ask your child what you did well and what you could do better.

- Ask for feedback about the specific steps of solving arguments.

Say to your child:

Practice

Now pretend that your teacher wants you to clean the chalkboards even though you just did it yesterday. Go through the steps of solving arguments.

- Practice solving arguments with your child, watching what he/she does to follow the steps. (For a description of practicing, see Chapter 3.)

- Tell your child what was done well and what to work on.

- Have your child practice until all the skill steps are followed correctly.

- Ask your child when this skill can be used at school or other places.

Dealing With Teasing

One of the hardest things for children to deal with is being teased, bugged, or laughed at by others. Teasing is usually a way of "pushing someone's buttons." Teasers know your child will react a certain way. They tease in order to elicit the expected response. When your child reacts the way teasers predict, their behavior is reinforced and the teasing continues.

Some children may not feel very good about themselves, and they tease to get attention. Others are jealous, and tease those who have talents or qualities they wish they had. Helping your child understand these reasons for teasing may help him/her remain in control and deal with it more effectively.

Help your child to realize that he/she cannot control the other person. All your child can do is control whether or not the teasing bothers him/her. If your child can control his/her own behavior by ignoring the teasing, telling himself/herself it's OK, or walking away, your child will send the message that he/she isn't going to give into or be controlled by the teaser. And, the teasing will likely stop.

> ### BOX 2-13
>
> ## SOLVING PROBLEMS: DEALING WITH TEASING
>
> **STEPS:**
>
> 1. Stop, take a deep breath, and count to five.
> 2. Decide what the problem is and how you feel.
> 3. Think about your choices and their consequences.
> 4. Decide on your best choice.
> 5. Do it.
>
> **DO:**
>
> ▶ Relax.
> ▶ Tell yourself to calm down and that it's OK.
> ▶ Think of at least three positive choices.
>
> **DON'T:**
>
> ▶ Yell, scream, or use inappropriate words.
> ▶ Call the other person names.
> ▶ Use negative comebacks.

The steps for dealing with teasing are listed with Do's and Don'ts in Box 2-13, as well as on Social Skills Card 10. More information for teaching the steps is covered in Chapter 3. When dealing with teasing, emphasize positive choices, such as:

▶ Ignoring the teasing.

- Walking away.

- Saying something good about yourself to yourself or to the other person.

- Telling yourself that the other person is wrong, so it's their problem.

- Saying how you feel in a friendly way.

Ask your child:

What does it mean to deal with teasing?

- To handle situations when other children make fun of something you say or do.

- To keep from losing control when someone bothers you.

Ask your child:

Why is it important to deal with teasing? In what situations would you use this skill?

- To remain in control and not let others "push your buttons."

- To feel good about yourself even if someone is trying to make you mad.

- To be able to think good things about yourself.

Say to your child:

Let's pretend that some children at school are teasing me because I got new glasses. This is what I would do. Watch closely and tell me which steps I use and which steps I forget.

- Demonstrate dealing with teasing by remembering all of the steps or forgetting some. (For a discussion of modeling, see Chapter 3.)

- Ask your child what you did well and what you could do better.

- Ask for feedback about the specific steps of dealing with teasing.

Say to your child:

Practice

Now pretend that some of your classmates are teasing you about making mistakes on homework. Go through the steps of dealing with teasing.

- Practice dealing with teasing with your child, watching what he/she does to follow the steps. (For a description of practicing, see Chapter 3.)

- Tell your child what was done well and what to work on.

- Have your child practice until all the skill steps are followed correctly.

- Ask your child when this skill can be used at school or other places.

Dealing With Being Left Out

All children want friends. Children often feel sad when they are left out of games or activities. Negative feelings about being excluded are normal, but how children handle their feelings can make a big difference in their lives. Over time, children might act out or say bad things about themselves—signs that they are internalizing how they are being treated.

Children leave others out for many reasons. They might not even realize that they're excluding your child or that he/she wants to play. Children also leave out others on purpose to make themselves look cool. Underlying reasons may be that they don't like themselves very much, or that they are jealous. Whatever the reason, your child can take certain steps when he/she is feeling left out. Emphasize positive choices when brainstorming choices and consequences, such as:

▶ Asking to join in.

▶ Saying how you feel using "I" statements.

▶ Playing with someone else.

▶ Doing something else that is fun.

▶ Telling yourself it's OK.

Example

Mia and Grace are playing in Mia's backyard. Nicole, Mia's neighbor, sees them through the fence and yells over "Hey! I'll be over in a minute to play with you!" Mia and Grace respond by saying: "We're playing with our Barbie™ dolls, and we only have two. We don't think you should come over." Nicole starts feeling sad and left out, and goes in the house ready to cry. Then she stops, takes a deep breath, and counts to five. She thinks to herself: "I'm feeling pretty left out because I was told that I couldn't play with Mia and Grace. Maybe I can get a Barbie™ of my own and bring it over. They still might tell me to go home. If they do, I'll just see if Morgan wants to play with me." Nicole then goes over to Mia's house with her Barbie™ and Grace and Mia say that she can play.

Suggestions for teaching this skill are in Chapter 3. Suggestions for what to do and what not to do are in Box 2-14, along with the steps for dealing with being left out. Use Social Skills Card 11 at the end of the book as an easy reference when practicing with your child.

Coach

Ask your child:

What does it mean to deal with being left out?

> To stay in control when other children leave you out of games and activities that you want to be part of.

> To think positive things when everyone else is doing something and you are not included.

BOX 2-14

SOLVING PROBLEMS: DEALING WITH BEING LEFT OUT

STEPS:

1. Stop, take a deep breath, and count to five.

2. Decide what the problem is and how you feel.

3. Think about choices and their consequences.

4. Decide on your best choice.

5. Do it.

DO:

> Relax.
> Use Body Basics.
> Think good thoughts about yourself.

DON'T:

> Pout.
> Call other people names.
> Interrupt other people.

Ask your child:

Why is it important to deal with being left out? In what situations would you use this skill?

- To remain in control if you don't get invited or included.

- To feel good about yourself even if you're not included.

- To be able to think good things about yourself.

List the skill steps and ask your child to repeat them.

Model

Say to your child:

Let's pretend that I was the last in your class chosen to be on a softball team. This is what I would do. Watch closely and tell me which steps I use and which steps I forget.

- Demonstrate dealing with being left out by remembering all of the steps or forgetting some.

- Ask your child what you did well and what you could do better.

- Ask for feedback about the specific steps of dealing with being left out.

Practice

Say to your child:

Now pretend that you didn't get invited to a classmate's birthday party. Go through the steps of dealing with being left out.

- Practice dealing with being left out with your child, watching what he/she does to follow the steps. (For a description of practicing, see Chapter 3.)

- Tell your child what he/she did well and what to work on.

- Have your child practice until all the skill steps are followed correctly.

- Ask your child when this skill can be used at school or other places.

Accepting "No"

Another difficult situation for many children is being told "no" when they ask other children to play, or when they want a privilege such as an extra serving of dessert or a special item at the store.

There are many good reasons children might be told "no." If children understand these reasons, they are usually better able to deal with the situation—friends might have other plans, teachers may want them to do something else.

Sometimes children need help understanding that parents and teachers are in charge and have the final word. This is often hard for children to accept, but it is important for them to learn to accept authority. As long as the requests adults make of children are reasonable, expect them to accept what they are told. Telling your child "no" using short and simple explanations is helpful, but do not engage in lengthy dialogues or debates. In this case, simple is better, and then move on.

When thinking about choices and consequences, emphasize positive choices, such as:

- Saying OK (accepting the answer).

- Saying how you feel in a friendly way by using "I" statements.

- Suggesting a compromise.

- Finding something else to do.

Steps for accepting "no" and Do's and Don'ts are listed in Box 2-15. For more details on the steps, review the section on solving problems. Teaching the steps of accepting "no" is discussed further in Chapter 3. Use Social Skills Card 12 at the back of the book as a handy reference when teaching your child how to accept "no."

Example

When Katrina says no to Stephanie, who asks to trade her lunch, Stephanie usually raises her voice and says how unfair Katrina is. As a result, Stephanie does not have many friends. Once Stephanie learns the steps, she is able to stop, take a deep breath, and count to five when Katrina says "no." She is able to think to herself: "I'm feeling disappointed because I cannot trade lunches. If I whine or argue, I might get my way now, but I won't feel happy when Katrina refuses to play with me at recess. I could just say OK and then we'd get along better." Stephanie accepts "no" and feels pretty good when she has fun with Katrina at recess later.

Ask your child:

Coach

What does it mean to accept "no?"

- To stay in control when you want something that you cannot have (such as extra money or a special privilege).

- To remain calm when you want to do something that you cannot do (such as spend the night at a friend's house or have extra time to do an assignment).

Ask your child:

Why is it important to accept "no"? In what situations would you use this skill?

- So other people can count on you to understand and not react negatively.

- To learn to deal with authority.

List the skill steps and ask your child to repeat them.

> ### BOX 2-15
>
> ## SOLVING PROBLEMS: ACCEPTING "NO"
>
> **STEPS:**
>
> 1. Stop, take a deep breath, and count to five.
> 2. Decide what the problem is and how you feel.
> 3. Think about your choices and their consequences.
> 4. Decide on your best choice.
> 5. Do it.
>
> **DO:**
> - Relax.
> - Tell yourself to be calm.
> - Tell yourself that it's OK.
>
> **DON'T:**
> - Pout, whine, or beg.
> - Talk back.
> - Yell at the other person.

Say to your child:

Let's pretend that my teacher told me I could not work on the computer, but I really want to. This is what I would do. Watch closely and tell me which steps I use and which steps I forget.

- ▶ Demonstrate accepting "no" by remembering all of the steps or forgetting some. (For a discussion of modeling, see Chapter 3.)

- ▶ Ask your child what you did well and what you could do better.

- ▶ Ask for feedback about the specific steps of accepting "no."

Say to your child:

Now pretend that your friend says that you cannot play with him at recess. Go through the steps of accepting "no."

- ▶ Practice accepting "no" with your child, watching what he/she does to follow the steps. (For a description of practicing, see Chapter 3.)

- ▶ Tell your child what was done well and what to work on.

- ▶ Have your child practice until all the skill steps are followed correctly.

- ▶ Ask your child when this skill can be used at school or other places.

Chapter 3

How Can I Help My Child Learn Social Skills?

There are many ways you can help your child learn social skills. The techniques covered in this chapter include coaching, modeling, practicing, and reinforcing (praising, setting goals, and making contracts). All of these techniques are useful for helping your child learn appropriate social behaviors. They are most effective when used in conjunction with each other. Chapter 4 discusses ways you can make sure that your child uses social skills when you're not around.

Refer to the Social Skills Cards at the back of the book when you work one-to-one with your child. The Social Skills Cards give suggestions for modeling and practicing with your child. Each skill that was reviewed in Chapter 2 has a corresponding Social Skills Card, so once you select the skill that you want to work on, you will have a "recipe" to guide you.

Although procedures such as coaching, modeling, and practicing may seem awkward at first, you will become more comfortable each time you use them. Try to relax, and have fun when trying these strategies with your child.

Coaching

Coaching is a tool for teaching children social skills. Just as a soccer coach teaches the rules and strategies for playing soccer, a social skills coach teaches the rules and strategies for appropriate social behaviors and lends support during practice.

How Do I Coach My Child?

To begin, you may want to explain to your child that there are steps for everything that they learn. There are steps for riding a bike, baking cookies, and solving a math problem. Similarly, there are steps to follow when playing with other children.

Depending on the age of your child, the time you spend teaching social skills steps in any one sitting will vary. Preschool children need lots of concrete examples using dolls or toys, and may be able to pay attention for only two or three minutes. Elementary-aged children, on the other hand, may grasp the concepts more easily by talking about them, and may pay attention for ten minutes or more. Older children can spend even more time.

As you coach your child, refer to the Social Skills Cards for quick reminders and to Chapter 2 for detailed explanations whenever you need help explaining skills or their steps. Box 3-1 provides the coaching steps at a glance. The "Checklist for Coaching" in the Appendix can be used as a guide as you are working with your child. After a coaching session, review the checklist to make sure you remembered all of the steps.

Take your time going through each of the coaching steps. Encourage your child to ask questions at any time and ask periodically if he/she has any questions. If your child does not understand a step or gets stuck coming up with ideas, go back and work on easier skills. Social skills tend to build on one another, (for example, a child must know about Body Basics in order to join in appropriately) and your child may not be ready yet for harder skills. Be ready to return to earlier skills if your child seems to be struggling.

BOX 3-1

HOW TO'S FOR PARENTS: COACHING

1. Introduce and define the skill.

2. Ask your child about situations in which to use the skill.

3. List the steps that are necessary to complete the skill.

4. Ask your child to say each step.

5. Post the steps in a visible place.

There are five basic steps for coaching your child in social skills:

1. **Introduce and define the skill.**

   Choose one skill to work on from Box 2-1 and spend time discussing it with your child. Define the skill as concretely as possible so that your child understands, and ask for your child's ideas on why the skill is important. If he/she cannot think of any ways the skill is important, share some of your own ideas. Definitions of each skill and ideas about why each skill is important are discussed in Chapter 2.

2. **Ask your child about situations in which to use the skill.**

   Try to engage your child in thinking about when the skill can be used. Give your child the chance to think about his/her friendships and to make sense of how social skills can be applied in his/her own life.

One way to get your child to start thinking about applying skills to real life problems is to ask about a real encounter in which the steps of a social skill could have been used. Situations may exist at school, at home, at the park, or any other place your child spends time.

If your child cannot think of any specific situations, try to guide the thinking process, but avoid making statements such as: "You always have problems with Kenny. You could use your problem-solving steps next time." This statement is not only too general (what is the specific problem?), but also decides for your child that there is a problem instead of letting him/her decide. The more your child makes decisions about which skills to use and when, the more he/she will "own" the problem, and the more likely he/she will try the steps. When your child "owns" a problem, he/she will be more willing to work toward finding an appropriate solution and will realize that he/she can control the problem by thinking of meaningful, personal alternatives.

It's a good idea to write down the situations your child comes up with. If he/she cannot think of any, suggest some of your own. Read the list back to your child and ask for any other ideas.

3. **List the steps that are necessary to complete each skill.**

    Provide the steps that go into performing the social skill from the corresponding Social Skills Card. When presenting the skill steps, make sure that your child knows what each one means. Refer to Chapter 2 for details on the skill and its steps. Use descriptions and explanations of each skill. You may need to repeat the steps once or twice to make sure your child understands their meaning. Sometimes having your child make a list on a separate paper or poster board is helpful to reinforce their understanding. Take your time discussing each step and be sure to answer any questions your child may have. For example, one of the skill steps for solving problems is thinking about choices and consequences. Does your child know what consequences are? Does he/she know that there may be both good and bad consequences to each possible choice? Some children think that consequences are only bad things that happen (such as, "If I don't mind my parents, I may get grounded"). They don't realize that appropriate behaviors can lead to positive consequences (such as, "If I mind my parents tonight, I may get to stay up later tomorrow").

4. **Ask your child to say each step.**

    Repeating each step in his/her own words will ensure that your child understands each one. You may ask your child to repeat them from memory, or read them from a list. If you are uncertain that your child understands, ask for examples of what he/she means. Go over each step until you are sure your child understands.

5. **Post the steps in a visible place.**

    At the end of the coaching session, post the Social Skills Card on the refrigerator, a wall in your child's bedroom, or another place where he/she will see it often. If your child cannot read, use pictures or other reminders of the skills.

Posting them in a visible place will serve as a visual cue to think about and practice good social skills. Keep each skill posted for about one week or until you think it's time to teach a new skill.

Example

Taylor is a seven-year-old girl who has difficulty starting conversations with others and inviting others to play. She wants to invite a friend, Holly, to her home on Saturday afternoon. Taylor's mother uses the following coaching dialogue to encourage her and make sure Taylor knows what to do:

"Taylor, I know you want to invite Holly over to play on Saturday. There are some things that you can do, or steps you can use, to start a conversation with Holly and ask her over. First, be sure to use the Body Basics (FEVER) that we talked about and practiced last week. Remember? They are: 'Face Holly, use Eye contact, use the right Voice, use a nice Expression, and Relax.' Go up to Holly and say hello, using her name, and decide what you want to say. Be sure to wait for the right time, when Holly is not busy talking to someone else or working. Since you want her to come over, you might say something like: 'Hi, Holly! Can you come over to my house to play on Saturday?'"

Modeling

Keep in mind that even with the best of discussions, some children (and adults, for that matter) remember things better when they are

Why Don't They Like Me?

demonstrated. Rather than stopping after a discussion of a particular skill, it's important to model the skill steps for your child. **Modeling** is acting out a skill using the skill steps in a particular context so that your child understands how the steps fit together and how the skill can be applied in his/her life. Showing your child how each skill is performed will make it more like real life, and more memorable.

Remember also that children learn by example almost all of the time. It's important to provide many, many examples of kindness, sharing, and caring in your own life.

How Do I Model Social Skills For My Child?

After choosing a skill and coaching your child in its specific skill steps, model the skill for your child by following the How To's for Parents: Modeling (Box 3-2). Also, perform the Modeling exercise on the back of the Social Skills Card (exercises also appear at the end of the skill sections in Chapter 2). The Checklist for Modeling included in the Appendix reviews the steps and can be used while you are working with your child. Also, it's a good idea to review the checklist after you model a skill to be sure you covered all the steps.

BOX 3-2

HOW TO'S FOR PARENTS: MODELING

1. Talk to your child about using the skill.

2. Express how important it is to pay attention.

3. Apply the skill steps to the example, leaving out one or two steps or applying them incorrectly.

4. Ask your child for feedback.

5. Repeat the example, completing all of the steps correctly.

6. Ask your child to report what he/she saw.

7. Make sure your child understands the skill steps.

As with coaching, take your time going through each of the steps and encourage your child to ask questions. If your child is not remembering the skill steps, go back to coaching until the steps are memorized. Then try modeling again.

There are seven steps to follow when modeling social skills for your child:

1. **Talk to your child about using the skill.**

   Discuss with your child a situation in which the skill can be used. It can be a situation that you discussed in a coaching session or a new one. It's best if your child comes up with the example because it will be more meaningful and memorable. If he/she cannot think of one, make up an example based on a situation you've witnessed, or use the Model example from the Skills Card (also listed at the end of that skill's section in Chapter 2).

2. **Express how important it is to pay attention.**

   Ask your child to pay special attention to the skill steps while you demonstrate. Indicate that once you are finished modeling, you expect your child to be able to tell you which steps were done well and which were done incorrectly or left out. This way, your child will be ready to provide feedback at the appropriate time.

3. **Apply the skill steps to the example, leaving out one or two steps or applying them incorrectly.**

   By leaving out some steps or applying them incorrectly, your child will have an opportunity to make comments about what was done incorrectly (or not done at all), and to report on what happened as a result. Believe it or not, your child will most likely be able to point out mistakes you make pretty readily. Most children enjoy giving adults feedback, and learn a lot from watching and commenting on inappropriate behaviors in these structured situations. It also gives them an opportunity to make suggestions about appropriate alternatives that can replace the inappropriate behaviors.

Example

Patrick has a hard time effectively dealing with situations when other children tease him. When modeling "dealing with teasing," Patrick's father first asks Patrick to tease him, and then begins arguing with Patrick and tries to tease him back. After about one minute of inappropriate behaviors, his father says "Time out! We're not getting anywhere. What did you see me doing?" Patrick immediately reports that his dad forgot the Body Basics, didn't stop to take a deep breath or think about choices, and did not make a good choice by arguing and teasing back. His father asks what he should have done, and Patrick gives explicit instructions to use a better voice, remain calm, and try ignoring the teasing or walking away. This gives Patrick's father a good opportunity to demonstrate the appropriate skill steps, using his son's suggestions.

Now they try the scenario again.

This time, when Patrick begins to tease, his father immediately takes a deep breath and counts silently to five. He waits a brief moment and then turns around and walks away. Patrick stops teasing, and his father again asks for feedback by saying "What did you see me do this time?" Patrick points out that he noticed his father taking a deep breath, staying calm, and walking away. His father asks him what happened next, and Patrick replies: "I stopped teasing because I wasn't getting anywhere!"

4. **Ask your child for feedback.**

Encourage your child to give you as much feedback as possible about what you did correctly (which steps you followed) and which steps you left out or didn't get quite right. Ask for a report on what your child saw. Ask questions such as:

- Did I use all of the skill steps?

- Which ones did you see me use?

- Were they used in the right way?

- Which did I do best?

- Could I improve how I did any of them?

- What should I have done differently?

- What would you have done?

Be sure to point out any mistakes that your child doesn't mention. If all of the steps were shown correctly, make sure your child knows this.

5. **Repeat the example, completing all of the steps correctly.**

    Your child needs to see the skill steps correctly applied to the example in order to learn how to use them. Contrasting correct and incorrect usage will deepen your child's understanding of social skills and help him/her to recognize mistakes later on, when he/she is attempting to apply the steps to real-life situations.

6. **Ask your child again to report what he/she saw.**

    Go over Step 4 again, asking questions to spark your child's thinking.

7. **Make sure your child understands the skill steps.**

    A good way of checking to see if your child understands is to ask that he/she say all of the steps. If necessary, show the skill again using another example.

Many skills are learned best when they are demonstrated. Social skills are no exception. Showing your child the steps that are included in the social skills that you are teaching provides another means by which to promote learning. It also provides an opportunity to have fun with the skills, since you can demonstrate some skill steps correctly and others incorrectly. It gives your child an opportunity to become involved in the learning because he/she can also report on what is observed and provide ideas to make social situations more effective. After coaching your child in the skill steps and modeling what they look like, it is then important to allow your child an opportunity to practice the skill. This is covered in the next section on practicing.

Practicing

Think about the last time you learned a new skill. Whatever it was—golfing, skiing, or playing an instrument—you might have read how-to materials or had an instructor describe the right moves. Was that enough to be sure that you could score a hole-in-one, ski an expert slope, or play a musical concerto without error? Probably not. You have to practice and practice until you get it right. Most people practice privately before going out in public, and when they do go out, they still make mistakes sometimes.

The same is true for social skills. Just knowing the skill steps is not enough for your child to perform them. Practicing the skills with your child first will prepare him/her to apply them to real-life situations. Your child will make mistakes along the way, but that's OK.

In modeling, you are the one performing the social skill being learned, but in **practicing** your child performs the skill or role plays. When your child practices, you can see clearly how well he/she is learning. Don't expect perfection the first few times. Practicing is a time for your child to test out new skills and get lots of helpful feedback and support from you.

How Do I Practice With My Child?

When your child is learning new skill steps, provide lots of opportunities for practice. Repetition will help your child be comfortable enough to use the steps when a real situation occurs.

Follow the How To's for Parents: Practicing (Box 3-3) when you practice with your child and use the Checklist for Practicing in the Appendix as a guide. Use the Social Skills Cards as a reference for the social skill steps. After a practice session, use the checklist to check your use of the practicing steps. Explain the Do's and Don'ts and ask your child to think of a situation in which the skill could have been used. Then, ask him/her to prac-tice (role play) the skill using all of the steps. Guide your child by ex-plaining that he/she should act as if the situation were truly occurring, and to practice the correct steps. If your child cannot think of an exam-ple to practice, use one provided on the Social Skills Cards (also at the end of each Skill section in Chapter 2).

As you practice, answer any ques-tions your child may have. Encour-age your child to take as much time as needed to feel comfortable with all the skill steps.

There are nine steps for practicing social skills with your child:

1. **Teach the social skill.**

    Choose a social skill to work on. Start by describing the social skill to your child, and coaching him/her using the coaching procedures in Box 3-1. Be sure to review all the steps listed on the Social Skills Card. Then model the skill for your child at least once by using the steps in Box 3-2.

BOX 3-3

HOW TO'S FOR PARENTS: PRACTICING

1. Teach the social skill.

2. Ask your child to think about using the skill.

3. Ask your child to describe the situation.

4. Begin the role play.

5. Act out the role of another child or person in the problem situation.

6. Continue the role play or stop action.

7. Give feedback about the performance.

8. Ask your child to try again, starting just before the point of difficulty.

9. Give additional feedback at the end.

2. **Ask your child to think about using the skill.**

   Once your child understands the skill steps and how they are performed, ask for an example of a time and place when the skill could be used. If your child is having difficulty thinking of a specific incident, ask questions to stimulate thought:

   ▸ What is one time that you could have used these steps with friends?

   ▸ Was there an incident in which this skill could have been used?

   ▸ Is there a common situation in which you can use this skill?

   If your child still cannot come up with any examples, supply one that you know of, or use a practice example from a Social Skills Card.

3. **Ask your child to describe the situation.**

   The effectiveness of the role play is determined partly by the degree to which the role play is realistic. Describing the problem in detail will set the stage for the role play and increase its meaningfulness. You can help your child get specific by asking questions such as:

   ▸ Who is involved?

   ▸ What is happening?

   ▸ What will they do?

4. **Begin the role play.**

   Explain that it is your child's turn to practice the skill, pretending that the situation is actually occurring. Make sure your child understands that he/she should try to use all the steps and to do the best job possible. Ask if he/she has any questions before you begin. Once your child understands what to do, start the role play by using a quick phrase such as "Action!" or "Go ahead." If your child responds slowly (or not at all), explain again how to start. Remind your child of the first few steps of the skill. If your child still doesn't respond, show the skill again. (See Box 3-2 for How To's.)

5. **Act out the role of another child, or person in the problem situation.**

   Make sure you understand the problem thoroughly so that you can provide a realistic role play for your child (see Step 3). Tell your child that you will be playing the part of another person who was present or might be present in the problem situation. The other person might be a child (such as a friend or sibling) or an adult (such as a teacher or even yourself). Try to take on the characteristics of the other person. For example, if you are acting the role of your child's teacher who you know is stern, try to be firm in your actions. If you are role playing the part of a neighborhood friend who is older than your child, use behaviors that depict this age difference (such as more mature mannerisms or language). Although this step may seem awkward at first, it is important that you try to make the role play as realistic as possible to increase its meaningfulness to your child. You may want to practice once or twice in front of a mirror or with another person (such as a friend or spouse) to become comfortable playing the role of another person.

6. **Continue the role play or stop action.**

   If your child uses the steps appropriately, allow him/her to finish the role play (go to Step 7). If your child fails to use the skill steps (i.e., begins to use ineffective or inappropriate behaviors), stop immediately. This is important because it provides an opportunity for your child to learn the specific problems that he/she is having, and the point at which they occur.

7. **Give feedback about the performance (what was done well, done incorrectly, or left out).**

   The main objectives of giving feedback are to support your child's attempts at using a skill and to provide suggestions for increasing the effectiveness of his/her actions. It is important that your child feels encouraged and supported in order to continue trying. Use the step of giving feedback as a chance to praise your child for trying and to recommend different behaviors that could be more effective for dealing with social situations or problems. When giving feedback, start with something that you noticed your child doing well. Then follow up with something that you would like your child to change, if there is anything that he/she did that needs improvement. Be sure to remain calm, positive, and consistent when giving feedback, so your child feels secure to try again and not fearful of being criticized.

8. **Ask your child to try again, starting just before the point of difficulty.**

    Let your child continue the role play until a mistake is made. If another step is left out or misapplied, stop the action again (repeat Step 6) and give feedback (Step 7). Proceed like this until all the social skill steps are acted out appropriately.

9. **Give additional feedback at the end.**

    Don't forget to point out what was done well and that your child was able to correct his/her own mistakes. Also mention which areas seem troublesome so that your child can try to focus on them next time.

Example

Pat is practicing solving an argument with her son Miguel. She is acting out the role of Miguel's friend Joshua. In the role play, Miguel and Joshua are having an argument and Pat yells at Miguel just as Joshua would. Because Miguel yells back instead of stopping, taking a breath, and counting to five (Step 1 of Solving Arguments/Box 2-12), Pat immediately says, "Cut!" and stops the role play. She praises Miguel for using eye contact, and reminds him of the step he's forgotten. Then she prompts Miguel to start the role play over. This time, when Pat yells at Miguel, he completes the steps successfully and Pat praises Miguel's efforts and his ability to follow all the steps.

Practicing is a very important component of teaching your child social skills. It allows your child to go through the steps of a social skill and try out different ways of acting in key situations. Do not be shy about practicing each skill several times with your child. Also, it is a good idea to encourage your child to use different choices or solutions while practicing so he/she gets an idea of how alternatives are performed. Like so many other skills, "practice makes perfect" when learning social skills! Practicing also gives your child confidence in his/her ability to perform difficult social behaviors competently. Some children simply do not think that they have the ability to control social situations, solve problems, or engage in other acts (and without teaching, some cannot). By having your child practice the skill steps, he/she will begin to realize that there are ways to make difficult situations more pleasurable, and that he/she can make that happen.

Positive Reinforcement

One of the most basic methods for increasing the use of social skills is reinforcement. **Positive reinforcement** is simply rewarding your child each time he/she demonstrates a desired behavior. This technique increases desired behaviors such as sharing toys, saying thank you, and being on time. Positive reinforcement can also be used to help your child use a new social skill more often (Sheridan & Dee, 1993). If your child tries to solve an argument with a friend by compromising rather than fighting, reinforce the behavior with a compliment and by granting a privilege (such as letting your child play with a special toy or have extra dessert). This encourages your child to compromise again next time.

How Do I Provide Positive Reinforcement?

There are many ways to provide positive reinforcement for your child. Some are simple and straightforward, such as praise. Others are a bit more complicated because they add elements to keep the reinforcement novel, meaningful, and effective. (Some specific guidelines will be provided in the following sections.) There are some basic components to using positive reinforcement when teaching your child social skills. They are: praising your child, giving rewards, drawing up a contract, and setting goals. Praising your child means providing positive verbal reinforcement when you notice your child doing something you like. Giving rewards means delivering a material reward or activity to your child when he/she engages in an appropriate behavior. Drawing up a contract means developing a written plan that you and your child agree to. The plan outlines expectations and rewards for when those expectations are met. Setting goals means establishing a plan with your child regarding the details of using a particular social skill (e.g., how often, with whom, in what location).

Praising Your Child

As you learn the most effective ways of praising your child, it's a good idea to periodically review How To's for Parents: Praising (Box 3-4). This will help you to keep in mind the qualities that make praise an effective reinforcer.

Examples of effective praise statements are in Box 3-5. Using statements such as these will help you discover the types of praise that work best with your child (Sheridan & Dee, 1993).

BOX 3-4

HOW TO'S FOR PARENTS: PRAISING

These five pointers can be remembered by the phrase "I FEED." Each letter of I FEED stands for a pointer:

▶ **I**mmediate Praise

▶ **F**requent Praise

▶ **E**nthusiastic Expression

▶ **E**ye Contact

▶ **D**escribe the Skill

Praising is most potent when it is frequent and enthusiastic and used "on the spot" as soon as a skill is performed. Being specific about the skill you are praising and making eye contact are equally important. As your child's social skills improve, all reinforcers, except praise, should gradually be removed.

It's easy to remember the main pointers for praising your child because the first letter of each spells I FEED (**I**mmediately, **F**requently, **E**nthusiastically, **E**ye contact, and **D**escribing the skill) (Rhode, Jenson, & Reavis, 1992).

Immediate Praise: Praise your child immediately "on the spot" when a social skill is used. The closer in time to the desired behavior, the more effective your praise will be. If you wait to praise your child, he/she may not know what you're praising, and may associate the praise with an unrelated behavior.

BOX 3-5

EFFECTIVE PRAISE STATEMENTS

Feel free to borrow from this list of praise statements when praising your child's social skills. Eventually, ideas will come more easily, and you will discover your own ways to praise your child.

- "You did a great job cooperating with Steve today! Thanks!"
- "Thank you for telling me about your problem with Karen on the playground today."
- "How great that you remembered how to start a conversation!"
- "Nice job asking Pei Fen to play with you and Sabrina!"
- "You two worked out that problem very well. I especially like the way you stayed calm and did not raise your voice! Good for you!"
- "Nice job thinking about solutions for solving that problem."
- "I'm really proud of you. I can tell you tried to use the problem-solving steps."
- "Thanks for sharing your toys with Wade today. You're a great sister!"
- "How wonderful! You used the steps of joining in!"

Why Don't They Like Me?

Frank's sons, who usually fight, are reading the rules of the game instead of arguing about who is right. Frank steps in right away, while his sons are still reading the rules, and says, "Hey, you two are solving your disagreement very calmly by reading the game rules! Way to go!"

Frequent Praise: Don't be stingy with praise! Giving lots of praise *every time* your child uses social skills is strong reinforcement. The more frequently you praise your child's skills, the better. Especially if your child is using a new skill, try to reinforce it every time it occurs.

Example

Frank notices that a second dispute arises over the game. Instead of yelling and calling each other names, the boys begin working out a compromise. Frank praises them again by saying, "You are really compromising and cooperating today. I'm very proud of you both."

Enthusiastic Expression: Be enthusiastic when you praise your child. Let your child know how truly happy you are with his/her use of social skills. Use superlatives (such as: great, fantastic, super, wonderful, excellent, amazing) to help convey emotion. This lets your child know how important good social skills are. It also helps your child feel good about himself/herself. When your child feels good about his or her skill use, using positive social skills on his/her own will be more likely to occur.

You notice that your daughter is ignoring her brother who is giving her a hard time about playing with dolls. You say "Erin, you're doing a FANTASTIC job ignoring your brother's teasing!" This is a much stronger reinforcer than "Good girl, Erin," which is vague and not enthusiastic.

Eye Contact: Make eye contact with your child when you are praising. Eye contact indicates that you really mean what you are saying.

It stresses the importance of your message because you take extra steps to look in your child's eyes. It also gets your child's attention, ensures that he/she hears and understands what you're saying, and allows you to check his/her response.

Six year old Stephan and his father were talking about what happened at school today. Stephan was obviously distraught when he told his father about a bully who intimidated him on the playground. Although Stephan did not have an immediate solution to the problem, his father was pleased that he was able to talk about it. Stephan's father touched his chin, lifted his face, and when Stephan was looking into his father's eyes, his father responded: "You did a nice job telling me about that difficult situation. I'm proud of you and how you talked about it!"

Describe the Skill: Clearly describe the social skill you are praising. Let your child know exactly what it is that he or she is doing that you are proud of. If your child does a good job overall with a skill like joining in, you can praise that general behavior. Sometimes, though, praising one important step such as "waiting for the right time" is important, especially if that step has caused difficulty in the past.

Example

When Cindy's mother says, "Great job!" Cindy is not sure exactly what she did that her mother is happy about. But when her mother says, "Cindy, you did a great job asking Megan to play with you," Cindy knows exactly what to do to garner further praise.

Rewarding Your Child

Everyone likes to be rewarded for a job well done. The same goes for your child. If he/she does a good job using social skills, consider rewarding your child with a "day off" from doing chores or an extra 30 minutes at the park.

Rewards are anything your child likes or enjoys. Every child is different, so what is reinforcing to one child may not be to another. Rewards might be objects (candy, stickers, toys) or activities (time with Grandma, a later bedtime, seeing a movie). They work best when they are used in conjunction with lots of praise.

Special privileges, activities, and praise are very reinforcing, so you don't need to "buy out the store" to keep your child motivated. Small rewards usually work just as well as big ones. Fun time spent with friends or family members is not only reinforcing, but also gives your child opportunities to use newfound social skills.

One way to make the process of choosing the reward easier is to brainstorm a Reward Menu. A **Reward Menu** is a list of possible rewards that you might be willing to provide. It should be realistic, excluding any ideas that you would never agree to, or that your child does not find appealing. It's best if the menu includes a variety of rewards (objects and activities) that range in strength of appeal. That way, you can start with smaller rewards that your child will enjoy and still encourage your child to work toward bigger items and privileges.

BOX 3-6

To get you going, a blank Reward Menu (Jenson, Rhode, & Reavis, 1994) is provided in the Appendix. It can be photocopied and used with your child. The sample Reward Menu (Box 3-6) may help you find ideas for your child's own menu.

Some parents and children like to select a reward in advance, others like to use variety and surprise. If spontaneity appeals to you, try writing rewards on slips of paper and letting your child draw one from a hat when it is earned, or use a spinner to see what is earned that day.

Whatever type of positive reinforcement you are using, there are some basic "rules" that should be adhered to:

1. **Reinforcers (or rewards) can be anything that your child likes, or finds desirable.**

   Be sure that what is selected as a reinforcer is something that your child truly wants. The reinforcer for engaging in an appropriate social behavior should be more appealing than whatever your child "gets" out of not performing the appropriate behavior.

2. **Change the reward frequently enough so that your child does not grow tired or bored.**

   Also allow your child to select bigger rewards to work toward.

3. **When you are teaching a new skill (one that your child does not know how to perform or that he/she performs infrequently), reinforce your child every time he/she uses it.**

   This lets your child know that performing the appropriate social skill correctly elicits a very pleasing response or event (i.e., receiving the reward).

4. **Once your child begins using the appropriate social skill regularly and effectively, gradually cut back on the frequency with which you give the reward.**

   This is important for three reasons. First, it will keep your child from becoming bored, and minimize the chance that the reinforcer will lose its appeal. Second, it is preferable for your child to perform appropriately on his/her own, without the need for constant reinforcement. Third, phasing out rewards will encourage your child to use the behavior more consistently and over a longer period of time. Because your child will not know exactly when a reward will be delivered, he/she will be encouraged to maximize the chance of earning a reward by continuing to use the social skill.

Drawing Up a Contract

A contract is a formal agreement between you and your child that describes the specific social skill that your child will use (e.g., solving problems, starting a conversation); the details around its use (e.g., when, with whom, how often); and consequences for its use (i.e., what will be earned).

Contracts with your child are fun, easy, and effective. In a social skills contract, your child agrees to use a new social skill a specified number of times during the week.

BOX 3-7

HOW-TO'S FOR PARENTS: DRAWING UP A CONTRACT

1. Select one specific social skill.

2. Find out how often the social skill is already being used.

3. Set a goal with your child.

4. Write down the details of the contract.

5. Keep track.

6. Review how well the contract is working.

7. Reward your child for meeting the goal.

In general, it is important that your contract be focused. Select only one skill to work on at a time and set a goal. Be precise about how often the social skill should occur and include details. The contract should spell out exactly what will be earned, when it will be earned, and how to keep track.

Contracts detail expectations, create a structure for your child to use and monitor specific skills, establish time frames for skill use, provide structure for discussion, and encourage your child to take responsibility in setting up expectations and following through.

Contracts are nice additions to reinforcement programs because of their flexibility. They can be used for essentially any behavior; they can be set up on any time frame (i.e., behaviors can be monitored daily, weekly, monthly, etc.); they can be combined with other forms of positive reinforcement (such as praise); they can be individualized; and they can be withdrawn or reintroduced at any time. When learning new social skills, a daily or weekly contract coupled with frequent praise is workable. That is, praise each occurrence of a new skill that you see your child using, keep track of the number of times that you see your child using the skill, ask your child to keep track of skill use on a separate or attached chart, and be ready to deliver the reward as soon as your child's goal is met.

There are six steps to drawing up a social skills contract with your child:

1. **Select one specific social skill.**

   Choose one social skill that you would like your child to use more often. Choose a positive skill your child can apply (such as accepting "no" as an answer); not a negative behavior that you want to decrease (e.g., arguing). Focusing on a positive skill is better than trying to decrease a behavior, because it tells your child what to do, or what to work on.

2. **Find out how often the social skill is already being used.**

   Keep a record of how often your child uses the social skill now so that you can clearly identify improvement. You can keep track of each time your child uses the skill by making marks on a chart, calendar, or sheet of paper. An example of a chart that you can use to keep track of social skills or other behaviors is contained in the Appendix. If your child never seems to use the skill, check to see if he/she knows the steps. If not, coach him/her again. (See Box 3-1.)

Even if you don't spend all day with your child, you probably have some opportunities to observe him/her using particular skills. Consider selecting one period of time that you spend regularly with your child (such as after breakfast or before dinner). Watch to see if your child uses his/her social skills at that time each day. If the behaviors are ones that occur at times when you are not present to observe them (e.g., asking others to play at recess or solving arguments in an after-school program), ask a responsible adult (teacher or monitor) for reports. You might also ask your child to keep track of what happens on a social skills chart.

3. **Set a goal with your child.**

   A goal is a specific behavior that your child will engage in to achieve desired outcomes. Goals can take many forms. For example, your child might set a goal to use a specific social skill (e.g., asking others to play) five times in one week. As part of that goal, he/she may specify when, where, and with whom this will occur (e.g., every day on the playground with children from the soccer team).

   The contract sets a goal, spelling out how many times your child will use the social skill during the week (e.g., "I will use the steps of playing cooperatively three times" or "I will play cooperatively with Jenny when she comes over on Saturday"). Be realistic. If your child does not use the social skill at all (e.g., always gets into a heated argument and never remains calm), the goal might be: "I will use my steps for solving arguments calmly once this week." If your child accomplishes the goal, he/she earns a reward from the Reward Menu. As your child begins to demonstrate the social skill more often or in different situations, you can "up the ante" and increase the number of times the skill must be used in order to get the reward.

Setting goals helps your child learn that he/she has control over his/her own behavior. Goals help your child "take ownership" of social skills and give your child the power to make behavioral changes. Your child will probably need help setting goals, deciding if the goals were met, and revising goals when necessary. A goal has two parts: an achievable objective and a deadline or time frame.

Encourage and expect your child to make his/her own decisions about what goals to set. Allowing your child to choose goals teaches him/her about making decisions and accepting consequences. It conveys to your child that he/she is responsible for his/her own choices and actions.

Sometimes children have unrealistic expectations and set a goal that is too difficult. Letting your child set his/her own goals as much as possible is essential, but you still need to guide your child so that he/she can succeed (Doll, Sheridan, and Law, 1990). Keep in mind that learning how to set realistic goals is not the objective, learning social skills is.

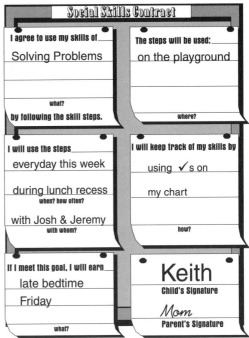

Social Skills Contract

I agree to use my skills of_____
Solving Problems

what?
by following the skill steps.

The steps will be used:_____
on the playground

where?

I will use the steps_____
everyday this week

during lunch recess
when? how often?

with Josh & Jeremy
with whom?

I will keep track of my skills by
using ✓s on

my chart

how?

If I meet this goal, I will earn_____
late bedtime

Friday

what?

Keith
Child's Signature

Mom
Parent's Signature

Figure 3-1

Setting goals is an essential part of the contract process (Doll et al., 1990). The steps for setting goals appear in Box 3-8.

4. **Write down the details of the contract.**

Use the blank contract provided in the Appendix or, if you prefer, write up your own contract following the example in Figure 3-1. The contract should include the expected skill, the time frame, frequency, how the skill will be tracked and by whom, and what the reward will be if successfully completed.

BOX 3-8

HOW TO'S FOR PARENTS:
SETTING GOALS

1. **Ask your child to state a goal.** When stating a goal, encourage your child to use an "I" statement. For example, if your child is learning the skill of starting a conversation, her initial goal might be: "I will call Melissa on the phone."

2. **Make sure the goal is specific, manageable, and positive.** In other words, the goal describes one specific action (such as inviting a friend to play) so that your child will know exactly what to do to meet it. Make sure the goal is one that your child can control, and that he/she will probably be successful in meeting. The goal also says what your child should do, rather than what your child should not do.

3. **Write down the goal on the contract.** Include **when** your child will attempt the goal (e.g., tomorrow afternoon), **where** (on the playground), and **with whom** (with Mary).

4. **Decide how to determine if the goal was completed.** Include a time frame for your child to complete the goal (e.g., by Monday) and the number of times a behavior must occur (three times this week) for completion of the goal.

5. **Check back.** After your child has had enough time to complete the goal, check to see how it went. If the goal is to perform a social skill several times a week (such as "I will solve arguments with Mary calmly three times this week"), check often to see how it's going. If your child doesn't seem to be making progress, you may need to change the goal so that he/she can be successful.

(adapted from Doll, Sheridan, and Law, 1989)

Why Don't They Like Me?

The contract should also be signed by you and your child. This makes it more "official" and adds to its importance. Having your child sign reminds him/her of the agreement. Your signature also indicates that *you* agree to the contract, and will follow through with a reward when the goal is met.

A week is generally a good time frame for a contract because it is long enough to give your child a chance to meet his/her goals, but not too long in case the goal was unattainable. If your child has difficulty attaining the goal, set a new one that may be easier.

5. **Keep track.**

Include in the written contract how you or your child will keep track of how often he/she uses the skill. Decide on a system for keeping track and follow through. You might tally how many times your child uses the skill by making check marks, coloring in squares, or putting stickers on a chart. A sample tally chart is included in the Appendix. You might also have your child keep a tally each time he/she uses the skill, but have a way to check the accuracy. For example, it's a good idea to set aside time each evening to discuss tally marks.

6. **Review how well the contract is working.**

After a few days, look at the information that has been collected in Step 5 and compare it to how often the skill was used before the contract started. If your child is using the social skill more often, keep drawing up contracts until the skill comes naturally to your child and is used consistently. Then gradually remove the contract. Draw up a contract every other week, then every three weeks, and so on, but remember to continue praising your child every time the skill is demonstrated. This will keep your child using the skill.

If you are not seeing an increase in skill use, make some changes to the contract. You might change your child's goal or spend more time discussing uses of the skill. Discuss any changes made to the contract with your child so that you both agree that the changes are important and fair.

7. **Reward your child for meeting the goal.**

One of the most important steps of setting up a contract is to follow through with rewards once they are earned. If you expect your child to keep working hard at learning and using new social skills, you must follow through on your end of the contract. If this doesn't happen, your child will quickly lose interest and stop trying different ways of behaving. Reward your child for meeting the goal as soon as it is completed. For example, if you and your child agreed on a goal for him/her to start at least three conversations with new playmates at school in one week, and your child meets the goal after three days, reward him/her as soon as possible. Do not wait the entire week before delivering the reward, and do not postpone delivery of the reward to some unspecified time. The reward will lose its strength, and the momentum will be lost. Immediately upon meeting the goal and earning the reward, establish another contract with your child. The new contract can focus on the same social skill, or it can cover a new skill that you are teaching.

The "Checklist for Drawing up a Contract" (Appendix) summarizes the steps of contracting and can be used to make sure you complete each step. Once you have used the checklist a couple of times and know how to set up contracts, you may find it useful as a reference.

This checklist provides a summary of the steps of contracting, and can be used when setting up a contract with your child to make sure that all of the important components are covered. The checklist can be used in two ways. The first few times you draw up a contract with your child, it might be helpful to have the checklist in front of you to serve as a guide. That way, you will be sure to cover each step. Then, when you are comfortable with the process of contracting, you can refer to it after you set up a contract to ensure that you remembered everything.

Using any of the positive reinforcement methods—praise, rewards, or contracts—will promote your child's use of social skills. You've probably heard the adage, "The whole is greater than the sum of its parts." This also applies to reinforcing your child. That is, each of the reinforcement techniques can be effective when used alone, but they are even more effective when they are used in combination. It is therefore important to try to be creative with reinforcement and use the various procedures in conjunction with each other.

Example

Praise is a good reinforcer by itself, but when praise is combined with another reinforcer, it is even more effective. Saying "I am proud of you for the way you controlled your temper just now" will reinforce the behavior. But adding, "I think that deserves extra ice cream after dinner" is much more powerful.

Marisol's contract states that she should use self-control at least three times in five days when playing with her two-year old brother (who frequently grabs toys and pushes). After three days Marisol's mother notices improvement, but sees that it may be difficult for her daughter to keep it up. She slips a piece of paper into her daughter's lunchbox that says: "You're doing a SUPER job using self-control with your younger brother. Here's a kiss to show how much I appreciate it!" Included in the lunch is a piece of chocolate candy "kiss."

Although contracts and reinforcement programs are formal, they should also be flexible. If you notice your child doing something really great that is not part of his/her contract (or that is not the same as the behavior you are trying to increase), be sure to praise the new behavior as well. For example, if you notice your child sharing his/her belongings or helping another child in need, let your child know that you noticed, and that you really like that kind of behavior.

Chapter 4
How Can I Help My Child Use the Skills Being Learned?

O nce your child starts learning social skills, you may think that is enough, and that your child will now be able to venture out and become a "social butterfly." Unfortunately, it's not that easy. In most cases, children will not use social skills on their own. They still need help noticing opportunities for practicing new skills. You can ensure the use of newly learned skills by reminding your child when opportunities arise, by supporting your child's friendships, by talking about friendships, and helping your child solve problems.

Reminding

Every day there will be opportunities for your child to use social skills. One of the most important things you can do to help your child use social skills is to remind him/her "on the spot" when it is a good time to practice. Let's say an argument comes up when your child is playing with a neighbor. Your child may not think of using the steps of solving arguments. That's the time to step in and remind your child to use the skill.

Parents sometimes feel that they're being a "busy body" when they interject in children's play. Just keep in mind that stepping in and reminding your child to use skill steps is the only way your child will learn to apply them.

Simply put, **reminding** is helping your child remember to use social skills in situations as they arise. When reminding, your job is to notice opportunities for your child to use appropriate social skills, and actively suggest that they do so.

How Do I Remind My Child?

One of the keys to transferring practice to real-life situations is to recognize opportunities for your child to use skills. Observing your child at play will give you the chance to step in and help him/her use skills "on the spot."

There are three strategies to help your child use social skills: reinforcing, prompting, and coaching/modeling. By using these three strategies every day, in real-life situations, your child is given the opportunities and support needed to use newly learned social skills. It is important to make these strategies part of your daily routine. **Reinforcing** lets your child know that you notice his/her attempts to use social skills, and that he/she is doing a good job. This increases the likelihood that your child will keep trying. **Prompting** is pointing out when a situation your child is in is appropriate for trying out a social skill. **Coaching/modeling** is reminding your child of the skill steps or demonstrating them when he or she doesn't remember how to perform a skill.

Jake has problems with his temper. In practice situations with his mother, Jake is able to stop, think about his problem, and identify a positive response such as "It's OK if I don't win this game," or "Justin played fair and square." But when Jake is playing with his friends and things don't go his way, he begins yelling, "This isn't fair!" and "You cheated!" Jake doesn't see the situation as an opportunity to use his skills of controlling anger. As soon as Jake raises his voice, his mother steps in and says, "Jake, this is a good time for you to use the steps of controlling anger." Even better, the next time a game is about to end, she steps in to remind Jake before he begins to raise his voice.

Reinforcing

Always reinforce your child in a positive way when he or she tries to use a social skill, even if your child has difficulty. This encourages your child to keep trying even when it is hard. Positive reinforcement can include rewards that your child can earn. For example, you might keep track of how many times your child solves disagreements calmly. Let your child know that you are keeping track. Points can be given each time your child uses a social skill until enough are earned for a small reward that you and your child have agreed on. Make sure your child understands exactly how many points are required to earn the reward. For reminders on goal-setting and contracting, see Chapter 3.

Praise is also important. Remember to praise each time your child tries to use social skills, not only when he/she gets them right. An example of praise to use "on the spot" is "Nice job working out that disagreement with your brother!"

Box 4-1 provides suggestions for reinforcing. It may also be helpful to review the section on positive reinforcement in Chapter 3 and the I FEED guidelines for praise in Box 3-4, if you need a refresher.

Prompting

Prompting is pointing out to your child situations in which a social skill can be used. Prompting can be done in two ways. First, you might tell your child in advance to remember to use the steps of a specific social skill when going to play with friends. Second, when your child is in a situation that requires use of a particular skill, you could step in and instruct him/her to use the skill at that time. This is important when you see that your child has an opportunity to use a skill but doesn't do so.

Be sure to use eye contact and a firm, positive (but not demanding) voice when prompting your child. If your child is in a problematic situation with friends, give him/her a chance to solve it before stepping in. If you see that your child is simply not trying to use the appropriate skill steps, or not using the steps accurately, remain as calm and neutral as possible when prompting.

You will not always see firsthand the problems your child encounters. In many cases you will simply hear about situations later when your child tells you. Praise your child when he or she tells you about an attempt to use a skill. If your child didn't try to use the skill steps, remind him/her of how the skill could have been used.

Box 4-2 provides suggestions for prompting your child. Examples of prompting statements include:

> "Today when you're on the school bus, remember to use your steps of starting a conversation."

> "I can see that there is a problem here. Let's try to use the problem-solving steps."

> "This is a good time to practice your steps of joining in. Do you remember what they are?"

BOX 4-2

SUGGESTIONS FOR REMINDING: PROMPTING

> Look for situations in which your child can use social skills.

> Prompt your child to use social skills.

> Your child may not follow your suggestion every time. Stay with your child until there is a plan to solve the problem.

Example

Hunter's father is watching Hunter and his friend Malcolm play basketball. When Hunter and Malcolm get into an argument about the rules, Hunter could use his problem-solving skills but doesn't remember to use them on his own. Hunter's father walks over to the boys and says,

"There seems to be a problem here. Now is a good time to use the problem-solving steps." When Hunter attempts to solve the problem, his father praises him by saying, "I really like how you tried to figure out a solution and decided to compromise. Great job."

Coaching/Modeling

Sometimes children don't try to use a skill even after prompting. When this happens, it is usually because they don't remember what the steps are or how to do them. Coaching or modeling the skill again usually helps. (Box 4-3 provides suggestions for coaching/modeling. For a refresher on coaching and modeling, refer to Chapter 3.)

When coaching your child in how to perform a skill, talk through the steps by saying things such as: "Remember to stop and take a deep breath, like this." Then model the steps while your child watches. After that, have your child go through the steps. This reviews the skill steps and gives your child the chance to practice the steps in a real-life situation.

> **BOX 4-3**
>
> **SUGGESTIONS FOR REMINDING: COACHING/MODELING**
>
> ▸ If your child doesn't remember or doesn't try all the steps, demonstrate what they are right then and there. Don't wait until later.
>
> ▸ Be sure that your child performs the steps you demonstrated. It is not enough for your child to watch you. Your child must also do it!
>
> ▸ Be brief and specific so that your child can return to playing.

If your child does not remember the skill steps, or doesn't know where to begin, first remind him/her of what the steps are. Then demonstrate the steps and ask your child to repeat them. Allow your child to go through the steps on his/her own and see how things work out. Remember to praise your child for trying and to give gentle feedback to correct missteps.

Examples of coaching/modeling statements to use "on the spot" include:

- "Watch how I use the steps of joining in. After I am finished, I want you to use the same steps."

- "This is how to use the problem-solving steps. Watch me, then you practice them."

Reminding Your Child to Use Social Skills: Bringing Together Reinforcing, Prompting, and Coaching/Modeling

1. Before your child goes out to be with friends (e.g., school, parties, homes), remind him/her to use specific social skills such as playing cooperatively and solving problems.

2. Watch your child when he/she is with others, keeping your eye open for opportunities in which your child can use positive social skills.

3. Praise your child every time you see him/her try to use social skills by saying something such as: "Nice job using (or trying to use) the steps of joining in!"

4. If an opportunity arises and your child doesn't try to use a skill, prompt him/her. Say something like: "This is a good time for you to try the steps of problem-solving."

   - If your child then tries to follow your advice and use the steps, praise him/her: "I like the way you tried using the steps of controlling anger!"

- If your child uses the steps appropriately, reinforce him/her: "Great job using the steps of problem solving!"

5. If your child doesn't try to use the skill after being prompted, or tries but isn't successful, remind him/her of the skill steps. Use a statement such as: "When you have an argument, stop, count to five, and think about your choices."

   - If your child then tries the skill steps, praise him/her: "I like the way you tried to use the steps of accepting no!"

   - If your child uses the steps successfully, praise him/her by saying: "Great job using the steps of playing cooperatively!"

   - If your child tries the skill but is unsuccessful, show how to use the skill by acting out the steps. Then tell your child to try the steps again.

6. If your child still doesn't try to use the skill, or tries and isn't successful, give specific instructions on how to use the skill in the future and suggest that your child use the skill later. For example, you could say: "When you lose a game, first stop and count to five. Then, think about your choices and the consequences. Why don't you try the steps of controlling anger later when you have the problem again?"

Script for Reminding

Below is a step-by-step script for reminding your child to use appropriate social skills. It will help you remind your child to use appropriate social skills "on the spot." A "smile" means your child used the skill successfully and you don't need to continue with the script. An arrow means continue to the next step. Use the script the first few times, or practice with it in front of a mirror until you're comfortable. With a little practice, your ability to prompt calmly and effectively will come naturally.

1. **Before playing or spending time with other children, tell your child to practice specific social skills.**

   Some examples of this kind of reminding are:

   ▸ "When Tanya gets here, I want you to use your steps for playing cooperatively."

   ▸ "Today on the playground, please remember to use your problem-solving and self-control steps." ➡

2. **Notice when your child has an opportunity to use a specific social skill.**

   If your child tries to use the skill steps and does so appropriately, praise and reinforce his/her good skills:

   ▸ "You did a great job solving the problem with Tyler!"

   ▸ "Excellent job controlling your anger in that situation." ☺

   If your child tries to use the skill steps but does so inappropriately, praise him/her for trying:

   ▸ "I like the way you tried to use problem-solving in this situation with Tyler!"

   ▸ "You tried to talk about your feelings. I'm proud of you." ☺

If your child does not try to use appropriate social skills, remind him/her to use them:

- ▸ "This is a good time for you to try the steps of accepting 'no'."

- ▸ "There seems to be a problem between you and Tyler. Why don't you try to use your problem-solving steps?" ➡

3. **See if your child tries to use the skill steps.**

If your child tries to use the skill steps and does so appropriately, praise and reinforce his/her good skills:

- ▸ "You did a super job solving the problem with Kristi!" ☺

If your child tries to use the skill steps but does so inappropriately, praise him/her for trying:

- ▸ "I like the way you tried to use self-control with Robby!" ☺

If your child does not try to use appropriate social skills even after prompting, tell your child the skill steps:

- ▸ "I want you to use the steps of accepting 'no'. Remember, the steps are..."

- ▸ "Use the steps of self-control when this happens. The steps are..." ➡

4. **See if your child tries to use the appropriate social skill after being told the steps.**

If your child tries to use the skill steps and does so appropriately, praise and reinforce your child's good skill use:

> ◗ "Great! Now you've got the steps of problem-solving down pat!" ☺

If your child tries to use the skill steps but does so inappropriately, praise your child for trying:

> ◗ "I like the way you tried to count to five and think about your choices." ☺

If your child doesn't try to use appropriate skills after being told the steps, model the appropriate skill steps:

> ◗ "Watch how I use the steps of joining in."

> ◗ "I'll practice the steps of playing cooperatively. Watch me." ➡

5. **See if your child tries to use social skills after being shown.**

If your child tries to use the skill steps and is successful, praise and reinforce your child:

> ◗ "Great! You really showed a lot of self-control that time!" ☺

If your child tries to use the skill steps but does so inappropriately, praise your child for trying:

> ◗ "I like the way you tried to stay calm and solve the argument with Stan." ☺

If your child does not try to use the skill steps after being shown suggest that your child try to use the skill steps later:

- "Next time this occurs, try the steps of solving problems."

- "You're having a difficult time with this right now. Let's practice later." ☺

Flowchart for Reminding

Each social situation your child experiences will be unique so what you do "on the spot" will vary. At times, your child will respond to simple reminders to use skills. Other times, direct prompts and modeling will be required. The Flowchart for Reminding (Figure 4-1) on the following page provides a visual representation of the reminding process. It shows the steps to take based on how your child responds. After you have a chance to use reminding with your child, check yourself by comparing what you did with the Checklist for Reminding in the Appendix.

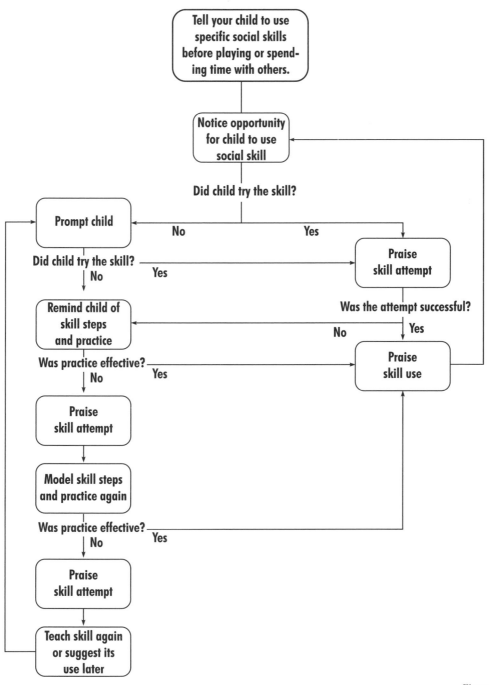

Figure 4-1

Supporting Your Child's Friendships

You can assist your child in making and keeping friends by increasing opportunities to play with other children. You can also show support by talking to your child about friendships, and helping your child solve his/her own problems.

Providing Social Opportunities

Sometimes children don't learn to get along and solve problems simply because they have not had many chances to try. By making sure your child has opportunities to play with others you are helping him/her learn to get along. Your child will learn many social skills from other children.

There are many reasons why some children do not play much with others. Some children spend the majority of their time watching TV or playing computer games by themselves. Others are reading or doing homework most of the time. Still others live in neighborhoods where there aren't many children. Whatever the reason, making an effort to have your child meet other children promotes his/her ability to make and keep friends. Playing with brothers and sisters is good, but it's not a substitute for playing with friends. Some ideas for providing social time are:

1. Limit the amount of time your child spends watching TV and playing computer or electronic games to two hours per day. Watching TV and playing computer games takes time away from social opportunities. Besides, much of what is on TV and in computer games is negative, aggressive, and violent. Try to limit these activities. Time allotted for TV watching or playing computer games may be increased slightly on weekends or holidays.

2. Make sure your child has board games and sports equipment that require at least two people to play. They don't need to be expensive or brand new.

3. When your child says that he/she is bored, suggest calling someone on the phone or going to a friend's house.

4. Set aside one or two days a week for your child to have a friend play at your house. This provides opportunities to play with other children and gives you the chance to see how well your child is getting along.

5. On family outings, ask your child to invite a friend. You might take your child's friend along to a favorite restaurant, park, museum, or shopping mall.

6. Talk with other parents about having your children get together. Share driving responsibilities to make sure that the children get back and forth safely.

7. Encourage your child to join structured groups or clubs, such as the Boy Scouts, Girl Scouts, or the 4-H Club. Taking dance lessons or playing on sports teams are also social activities. Local libraries and parks often have structured activities on weekends or summer days that will allow your child to try a new hobby or craft.

8. Take your child to places where other children like to go: zoos, water parks, museums, and movies. Parks often have swings, slides, and climbing bars for children of various ages. Parks provide a fun and inexpensive outing for you and your child.

9. When arranging play dates for your child, keep in mind that it's best when children are about the same age. That way, your child learns skills that are appropriate for his/her grade and age. Socializing with children who are older or younger is OK some of the time, but it doesn't take the place of same-age play.

Talking to Your Child About Friendships

Because children spend so much time with friends in school and away from home, it is often difficult for parents to understand the problems their children face each day. Many children believe that they will get into trouble at home for what happens at school, that their parents don't understand their problems, or that their parents are not interested in their friendships, (Doll et al., 1989).

Most parents want to help their children. But even with the best intentions, sometimes parents don't seem supportive of their children's social experiences and friendships. Talking to your child about friendships is a powerful way to show you care. How you go about talking to your child is as important as setting the time to do it. This section provides basic guidelines for talking about friendships and points out some of the common pitfalls.

Sometimes parents try to solve problems quickly because they feel like they should have all the answers instantly. Or, parents might act as if their children's problems are not a big deal or not really a problem. Unfortunately, parents don't always look beyond the surface and try to understand problems, so it continues to cause their children stress.

Curtis sometimes has problems getting along at the playground. When he is left out of a game or not included on a team, he calls the children names and gets into a verbal battle. After school he comes home and tells his mother what happened. Because it's not the first time he's had such a problem, she responds by saying "What did you do this time?" This makes Curtis feel more frustrated. By not finding out what the problem really is, and how Curtis is feeling, his mom conveys the message that his feelings don't matter.

Next time, when Curtis's mom says "You seem upset about what happened on the playground. Why don't you tell me about it?" Curtis is able to explain the situation and provide information to solve the problem.

Some of the common things parents say are interpreted by their children as preaching, lecturing, criticizing, interrogating, or ordering. For example, telling your child what to do or questioning your child's motives are common pitfalls. Jumping to conclusions, interrupting your child, or telling him/her how to feel leaves a feeling of being misunderstood and doesn't help your child learn to solve problems. (Doll et al., 1989). Help your child feel supported and comfortable by letting him/her know that you care about friendships. Try to be open and encouraging, and avoid lecturing or passing judgment. Setting aside time to truly listen to your child communicates that what he/she feels and says matters to you.

Keep in mind that you may not solve the problem right away. The first step is to show your child that you truly care about his/her feelings and friendships. You can indicate your care, support, and respect by remaining calm, nodding and smiling, and leaning toward your child.

How Do I Talk to My Child About Friendships?

Parents can help their children to solve problems with peers by calmly discussing problems and listening carefully. When talking with your child about social skills, take your time. You can learn what is troubling your child by helping him/her notice and talk about feelings. This also sets the stage for your child to solve his/her own problems.

Help your child discuss actions and feelings by encouraging the use of "I" statements: "I feel sorry about the fight I had with Mike" (not "Mike makes me so mad when he acts like that!").

"I" statements help your child to take ownership of his/her actions and feelings. When your child "owns" a problem, he/she is in a position to do something about it (after all, your child cannot control others' behaviors, but only his/her own behaviors). When you direct your child to use "I" statements, you are helping him/her to find personal solutions instead of relying on you for answers. Your child can also begin paying attention to what really happened, instead of what you will think of him/her. "I" statements are described in more detail in Chapter 2.

Be open and encouraging when talking to your child about friendships. Avoid lecturing, interrogating, and judging and keep your comments brief so that your child can talk. Counting to five before answering your child will give you time to think about what he/she is saying before you answer. It also conveys that you are listening; that you understand and care.

There are six steps for talking to your child about friendships:

1. **Find the right time and place.**

   Make sure your child is ready to talk by finding the right time and place, and by "reading" your child's mood. Times when *you* feel like talking aren't always the times your child feels like talking. Make sure your child is in the right frame of mind. When your child is throwing a temper tantrum because a friend said she wouldn't play is not the time to talk about it. Let your child know that you are ready to talk when he/she is. When the tantrum has ended and your child is calm, talking will be more productive.

   The right place is also important. It's not a good idea to try to talk to your child about sensitive matters in a crowded mall or in front of friends. Rather, wait until you have some un-interrupted time and space together. Many parents find that before bed when their child is settling in, or in the car to and from school, are good options for talking to their children.

2. **Provide an opportunity for your child to talk.**

   Invite your child to talk to you about an event. Encourage your child to talk about thoughts and feelings, without ex-pressing your own. The event your child shares can be posi-tive, such as coming home with an A+ on a spelling test, or it can be difficult, such as a fight with a friend over a game of checkers. Examples of providing an opportunity for your child to talk include:

- "You're coming home from Sally's house pretty up-set. Let's talk about it."

- "I can see that you're proud of something. Please fill me in!"

3. **If your child doesn't respond to your invitation to talk, ask again.**

   Remember that your child may not be ready to talk or may need more encouragement:

   - "Why don't we talk about it?"

   - "I've got an open ear. Let's talk!"

   If your child still does not talk, cue for later. Convey that you are ready and willing to talk whenever he/she is. This re-assures your child that you care and will still be available later. Examples of cueing for later include:

   - "I'd really like to hear about what happened at Sally's whenever you feel like talking."

   - "You may not feel like talking about it now, but when you do, I'll be here."

4. **Keep your child talking by being a supportive listener.**

   Once your child begins talking, your objective is to *keep* him/her talking. You can do this by being a supportive lis-tener. Being a supportive listener means that you don't judge, but rather reflect your child's feelings, turning the dis-cussion back to your child quickly. This type of listening helps children learn about their feelings, encourages

Why Don't They Like Me?

children to solve their own problems, and may improve your relationship.

Asking open-ended questions is a good way to keep your child talking. Open-ended questions are ones that your child must respond to with a long response, rather than yes or no. "What happened then?" is an open-ended question that requires your child to describe the situation more fully. "Did you hit him back?" is not open-ended and requires a yes or no response. Examples of open-ended questions include:

- "What happened then?"

- "Describe what Yana did during recess."

- "Explain what you mean."

- "Tell me more about it."

Another way to keep your child talking is to restate the main ideas of what your child is saying. **Restating** is picking out the words that seem most important to your child, including feelings or ideas, and repeating them in your own words. It is best to keep these to a single sentence. Examples of restating include:

- "You were pretty upset when Rachel told you she didn't want to be your friend anymore."

- "You're feeling sad about what you said to Michael."

Brief words and body signs such as nodding, smiling, and leaning toward your child signal that you are listening. Body signs keep your child talking because they don't interrupt.

They say to your child: "It's OK to talk—I'm with you." Examples include:

▸ "Mm-hmm," (while nodding).

▸ "Really?" (while smiling).

▸ "Uh-huh," (while leaning toward your child).

5. **Acknowledge your child's feelings and actions.**

Let your child know that you understand his/her opinions. When your child shares problems with you, show that you understand by mentioning your child's feelings, actions, or opinions in your response. Examples include:

▸ "I understand how you were hurt when Martha said that you weren't good enough to be on her team."

▸ "I know how you feel."

6. **Begin problem-solving now or later.**

Keep talking to your child until the situation and his/her feelings have been described in detail, or until your child no longer wishes to talk. Most children have short attention spans and can only carry on a

---

BOX 4-4

HOW TO'S FOR PARENTS: TALKING TO YOUR CHILD

1. Find the right time and place.

2. Provide an opportunity for your child to talk.

3. If your child does not respond:
   ▸ Ask again.
   ▸ Cue for later.

4. Keep your child talking by:
   ▸ Using open-ended questions.
   ▸ Restating main ideas and feelings.
   ▸ Using brief words and body language to show you're listening.

conversation like this for five or ten minutes. (The length of time that your child is able to talk with you in this way depends on age and level of development.)

If you believe that your child has explained the situation and expressed his/her feelings completely, help your child begin the steps of problem-solving. To begin, use statements like:

▸ "This seems to be a real problem for you. What is the problem exactly?"

▸ "I'm sorry to hear that you are having such a hard time. What do you think the problem is?"

If you feel that your child is not able to continue talking, and that it is necessary to discuss the problem at a different time, cue your child to begin problem-solving later by using such statements as:

▸ "Thank you for talking to me about your problems with Jeff. Let's talk later about what can be done."

▸ "I hope that you feel better. Later on, let's talk about how to solve that problem."

Box 4-4 contains the steps for talking with your child. In addition, a script for talking to your child and solving problems appears at the end of this chapter. This script will help to put together all the pieces of talking to your child. It also provides examples of conversation questions and depicts the natural flow of discussion. Once you have tried talking to your child and solving problems using the steps in this section, it's a good idea to use the checklist in the Appendix to see if any of the steps were left out. If so, keep them in mind for your next talk.

Problem-Solving

Talking to your child is often not enough to help him/her solve problems. In most situations, it is necessary to encourage the use of problem-solving skills. Solving problems with your child involves talking about a specific problem, discussing various solutions, and taking action to solve the problem (Doll et al., 1989).

The goal of problem-solving is to help your child learn and use specific steps for dealing with a problem on his/her own. Your child needs to take responsibility for the problem and for choosing the best solution. There are specific steps suggested by many authors (Spivack & Shure, 1974; Weissberg, Gesten, Liebenstein, Doherty-Schmid, & Hutton, 1980) to help children solve their own problems. In general, they are:

- Identify a specific problem. (What is the problem?)

- Explore choices to solve the problem. (What are the choices?)

- Consider the consequences of each choice. (What are the consequences of each choice?)

- Select the best alternative. (What is my best choice?)

- Act it out. (How did I do?)

The steps of problem-solving (also presented in Chapter 2) allow your child to act on his/her own and learn how to make appropriate decisions. The help and approval your child needs from you or other adults will decline over time. Children feel good about themselves when they solve a problem on their own.

How Do I Help My Child Solve Problems?

Encourage your child to use the problem-solving steps by providing an open invitation to talk about a problem. Help your child to remain focused on the topic. Once your child is finished describing the situation and expressing all his/her feelings, begin the problem-solving sequence. Say something like: "This seems to be a real problem for you. What exactly is the problem?" This helps your child clarify the dilemma. You can help guide your child through the steps by following up with questions such as: "What are some of your choices for solving the problem?" and "What might happen if you do that?"

There are seven steps to keep in mind when helping your child solve problems:

1. **Talk about the situation and your child's feelings.**

   Begin problem-solving by talking calmly and being supportive. Learn as much as you can about the problem from your child's own words. Use supportive listening skills, letting your child tell the story and how he/she feels. Avoid making judgments or pressuring your child. Once you are sure your child is finished sharing, suggest that there is a problem to be solved.

2. **Identify the problem.**

   Once your child has finished discussing his/her feelings and actions, start problem-solving with a question such as: "What do you think the problem is?" Spend time helping your child define the problem. The more your child thinks through a problem, the more effective his/her solutions will be. Ask your child to state the exact problem in one or two sentences. The description should include what happened, with whom, and when. Examples of helping your child identify the problem include:

> ▸ "It sounds like you and Tina had a problem while playing at recess. Tell me in your own words what the problem was."

> ▸ "So the problem is that you and Tina fought about who used the jump rope the most times. She grabbed the jump rope and went to play with the other girls."

3. **Think about the choices.**

Let your child brainstorm as many choices as possible. Help your child come up with at least three solutions. If your child is not able to come up with three choices on his/her own, or if all your child's ideas seem inappropriate (e.g., they involve fighting), help by suggesting some others. To encourage thinking about choices, use statements such as:

> ▸ "What are some ideas you have that would help solve the problem with Tina?"

> ▸ "What do you think you could do when Tina starts to tease you?"

4. **Consider the consequences of each choice.**

   Help your child recognize both the positive and negative results of each choice. Also help your child think not only of immediate outcomes, but also of long-term results (e.g., telling the teacher about being teased may solve a problem immediately, but the long-term effect might be that the other children call your child a tattletale). If your child is unable to think of any outcomes, suggest some of your own. Examples of helping your child consider the consequences of choices include:

   ▸ "You said that one choice is to find someone else to play with. What do you think might happen if you did this?"

   ▸ "Another choice you suggested was to tell your teacher. What might happen if you did this?"

5. **Decide on the best choice.**

   After considering the possible consequences of each choice, allow your child to decide which choice is best. "Best" will vary according to circumstances, but should always be a choice your child believes in doing, and that he/she thinks will produce the most favorable results. In other words, let it be your child's decision, not yours. Encourage your child to follow through on his/her "best" choice, even if you don't agree that it's the best one (unless, of course, it is harmful to your child or to others). Your child will learn most from the problem-solving process when given free rein to make decisions.

To help your child decide which choice is best, use comments such as:

- "Knowing the good and bad consequences of each of your choices, which do you think is the best choice for you?"

- "So you could ignore Liza, find someone else to play with, or tell your teacher that she is calling you names. And you know what might happen if you did any one of these. Which do you think is your best choice?"

Help your child explore various choices to solve a problem and the likely outcome of each of the choices. Then allow *your child* to select the best choice. This not only shows support for your child, but also helps your child learn how to analyze choices. Your child will learn much more by exploring various options, making his/her own choice, and experiencing the consequences of that choice.

6. **Set a goal.**

Once your child decides which choice is best, help him/her to state exactly what action will be taken, with whom, where, and when. Following the steps and guidelines in Chapter 3 will make setting goals easier.

Examples of setting a goal with your child include:

- "So you decided to tell Jamie that your feelings were hurt when she didn't walk home from school with you. Let's set a goal that describes when, how, and where you will tell her how you felt."

▸ "OK, so you think that ignoring Sam when he teases you about your new brace is the best choice. How can we make that into a goal so that you are clear about how, when, and where you will ignore his teasing?"

7. **Check back.**

Once your child has had an opportunity to act on his/her best choice, discuss how it went. Let your child explain what happened, how the choice worked out, and how he/she feels. Be sure to praise your child for trying to solve the problem. If the choice did not work out, help your child go through the problem-solving steps again by rethinking the possible choices and their positive and negative outcomes. Again, let your child select the best choice. Evaluate the choice after he/she tries it.

Examples of checking back with your child include:

▸ "You were going to suggest to Austin that the two of you look up the rules of Chinese checkers to know who goes first. How did that go?"

▸ "How did it go when you played soccer with Trevor today? Were you able to ignore him when he yelled at all the players?"

Script for Talking to Your Child and Solving Problems

This step-by-step script for talking to your child and solving problems provides examples and suggestions for opening the conversation, keeping your child talking, exploring choices and consequences, and more. You may find the script helpful the first few times you talk and problem solve with your child. Over time, these steps will come easily and you will be able to converse openly and naturally with your child. A "smile" indicates that the script may end at that point. An arrow means continue to the next step.

1. **Start by asking your child about a situation or about his/her feelings:**

   ‣ "You seem pretty upset. Let's talk about it."

   ‣ "How did it go playing with Luis today?" *Ù*

2. **See how your child responds.**

   If your child does not answer, or responds in a way that is not very clear (says "no" or "fine"), repeat the question in a different way:

   ‣ "Why don't we talk about what happened?"

   ‣ "I'd like to hear about your school day." →

   If your child still does not answer, tell him/her you would like to talk later:

   ‣ "I'd really like to talk to you about your playtime with Luis. I'll be here when you're ready to talk."

   ‣ "If you feel like telling me about it later today, I'll be in the living room."

   ‣ "Let's try to talk about it later, when you are a little calmer." ☺

If your child answers, keep your child talking. Use open-ended questions:

▸ "What happened next?"

▸ "Tell me more." ➤

Restate your child's main ideas and feelings:

▸ "You were upset when Jorge kept picking on you."

▸ "You seem pretty frustrated."

▸ "They said some mean things to you." ➤

Use brief words and body language to show you're listening:

▸ "Uh-huh…. Mm-hmm…. Really?"

▸ "I understand." ➤

3. **When your child has finished telling his/her thoughts, use understanding statements:**

▸ "I understand how you would feel angry about what Luis did."

▸ "I can see how you would react that way." ➤

4. **Help your child identify the main problem:**

▸ "It sounds like you're really concerned. What exactly is the problem?"

▸ "So you feel angry and disappointed. What is the exact problem that you are having?" ➤

5. **Help your child think of at least three possible solutions:**

   ▸ "What do you think you can do about that?"

   ▸ "What else?"

   ▸ "What's another choice?" ➤

6. **Help your child consider the consequences of each possible solution:**

   ▸ "What do you think might happen if you decide to...?"

   ▸ "What might be the result of...?" ➤

7. **Help your child decide on the best choice:**

   ▸ "We talked about lots of choices, including.... What do you think is your best choice?"

   ▸ "Now that you've thought of all those choices, which one do you think is best?" ➤

8. **Help your child set a goal that is specific, manageable, and positive:**

   ▸ "You've decided to tell Monica that you feel hurt when she leaves you out of a game. Now make a goal for yourself, beginning with 'I will'." ➤

9. **Write down, or have your child write down the goal:**

   ▸ "Let's write down your goal so that we can both remember it. We will include when, with whom, and where you will try to meet your goal." ➤

10. **Check back later to see how things went:**

> "You decided to.... How did it work out?"

> "Are you satisfied with how the problem got solved?" ➙

If it went well, praise your child for how he/she handled the situation:

> "I like the way you tried to use problem-solving in this situation." ☺

If your child had some problems, praise him/her for trying and go through the problem-solving steps again if necessary:

> "It sounds like you still have a problem. What are some other possible solutions?"

> "What might happen if you choose...? What is your best choice?" ☺

Flowchart for Solving Problems

Because each of your child's experiences and moods is distinct, it is essential that your discussions be accommodating. At times, your child will be ready to talk openly and freely, talking through feelings and actions easily and completely. Other times, your child will seem more closed and quiet and will need encouragement to talk. In each situation, what you say and do in response will change. The Flowchart for Solving Problems (Figure 4-2) on the following page is a map of the problem-solving process. The order in which you follow the steps is based on your child's responses.

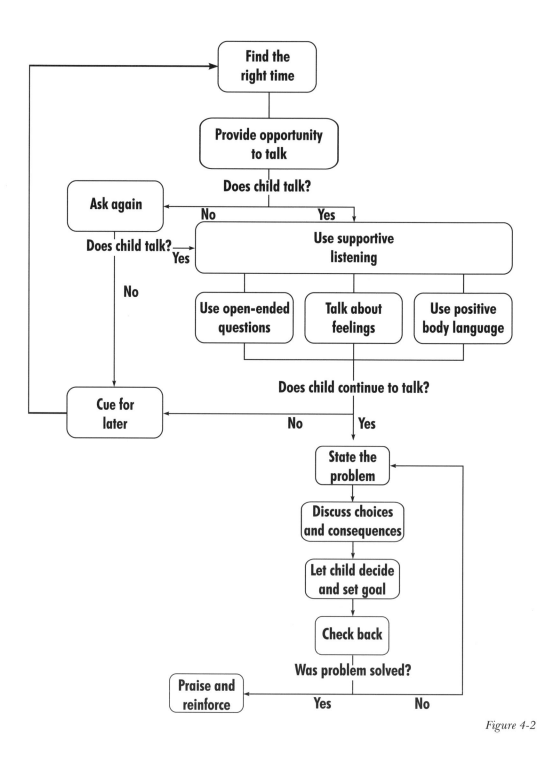

Figure 4-2

Conclusion

This book provides information and tools to help you work with your child in developing better social skills. As your child masters specific skills for beginning interactions, Keeping It Going, and Solving Problems, feel free to introduce new and different skills. This can easily be done by listing the important steps and using the techniques for coaching, modeling, and practicing.

Your ability to use these techniques, as well as prompting, talking, and problem-solving, will continue to improve as you use the checklists, scripts, flowcharts, and Social Skills Cards. Once you learn the basic techniques, you will probably develop your own style of using them, and that is good! The more you can incorporate the strategies into natural, daily interactions with your child, the better your child will be at using social skills everyday. Remember to stay calm, keep trying, and have fun!

It is likely that your child's needs will change over time. It's a good idea to review the skills and techniques in this book periodically as a refresher when working with your child.

You may also want to review some points on a regular basis (such as the first day of each month). As your child goes through transitions (such as beginning a new grade, establishing new friendships, or entering a new phase such as adolescence), extra time may be necessary to re-teach and reinforce specific skills. Be sure to make any adjustments that are necessary so that the skills make sense for your child. Change some of the wording if it seems too "childish" or if other words seem to make more sense to your child.

It is possible that difficulties may remain even with all the work, effort, and teaching you do with your child. Some children and parents simply need more individualized, professional attention to effectively address their difficulties. If your child continues to have problems socially after going through the strategies outlined in this book, you are strongly encouraged to contact your child's school for help. Getting the special help that you and your child need is an opportunity to make important changes in your lives. When you contact the school, ask if a school psychologist is available to meet with you. School psychologists are usually well-trained in procedures such as those presented in this book (social skills training, parent training, reinforcing, contracting). Additionally, school psychologists can often provide insights into the unique situations and challenges encountered by your child in the school setting. Alternative sources for help may be found at local children's hospitals, mental health agencies, and support groups (such as local chapters of CHADD, a support group for children and adults with attention deficit hyperactivity disorder).

You have made an important decision to help your child get along better with other children and adults. The social skills that you teach your child will make a big difference in your child's life. Similarly, the strategies that you learn to use to help your child can be used in many situations as your child grows. Good luck in all of your efforts, and keep smiling!

Appendix

- Reward Menu

- Social Skills Contract

- Checklist for Talking to Your Child

- Checklist for Reminding

- Checklist for Practicing

- Checklist for Drawing Up a Contract

- Checklist for Modeling

- Checklist for Coaching

- Social Skills Chart

- My Tally Chart

REWARD MENU

1

2

3

4

5

6

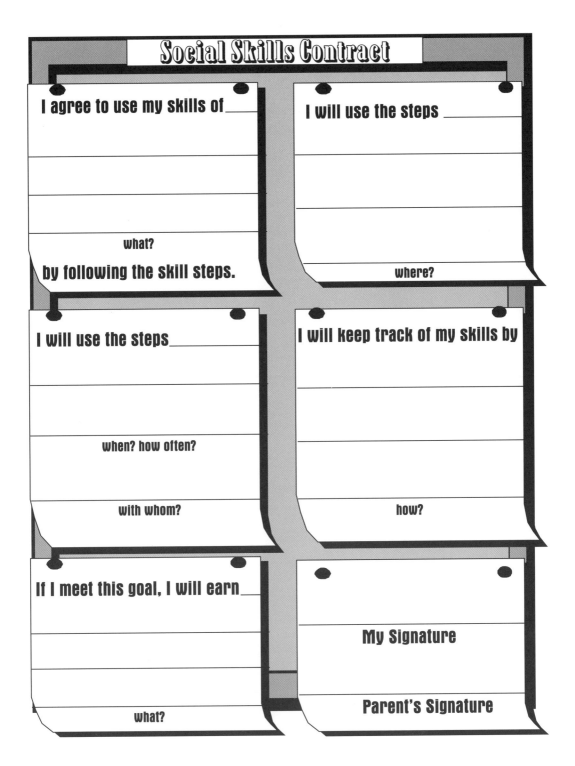

Social Skills Contract

I agree to use my skills of _____

_____

_____

_____

what?

by following the skill steps.

I will use the steps _____

_____

_____

_____

where?

I will use the steps _____

_____

_____

when? how often?

_____

with whom?

I will keep track of my skills by _____

_____

_____

_____

_____

how?

If I meet this goal, I will earn _____

_____

_____

_____

what?

_____

My Signature

_____

Parent's Signature

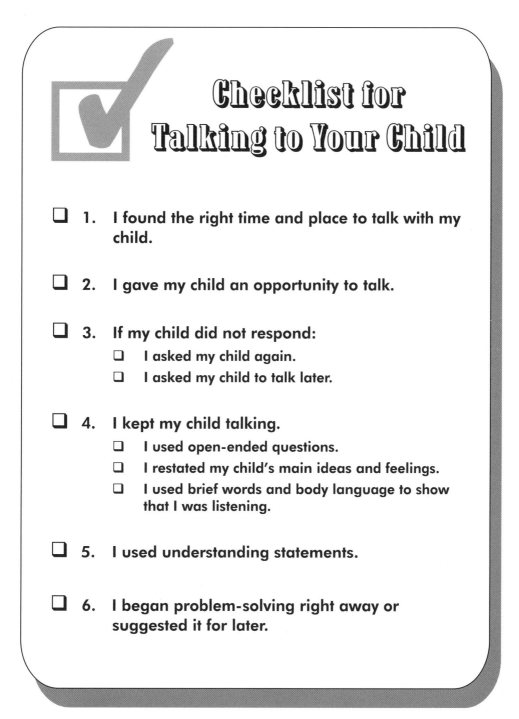

Checklist for Talking to Your Child

❑ 1. I found the right time and place to talk with my child.

❑ 2. I gave my child an opportunity to talk.

❑ 3. If my child did not respond:
   ❑ I asked my child again.
   ❑ I asked my child to talk later.

❑ 4. I kept my child talking.
   ❑ I used open-ended questions.
   ❑ I restated my child's main ideas and feelings.
   ❑ I used brief words and body language to show that I was listening.

❑ 5. I used understanding statements.

❑ 6. I began problem-solving right away or suggested it for later.

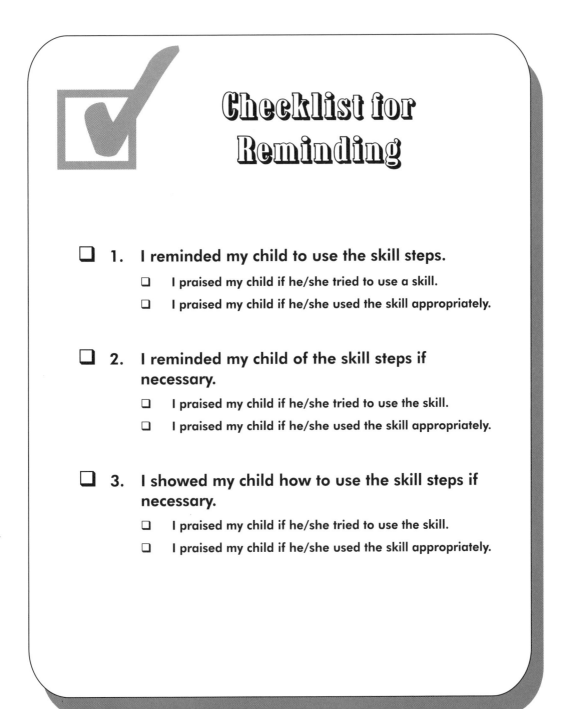

Checklist for Reminding

❑ 1. **I reminded my child to use the skill steps.**

    ❑   I praised my child if he/she tried to use a skill.

    ❑   I praised my child if he/she used the skill appropriately.

❑ 2. **I reminded my child of the skill steps if necessary.**

    ❑   I praised my child if he/she tried to use the skill.

    ❑   I praised my child if he/she used the skill appropriately.

❑ 3. **I showed my child how to use the skill steps if necessary.**

    ❑   I praised my child if he/she tried to use the skill.

    ❑   I praised my child if he/she used the skill appropriately.

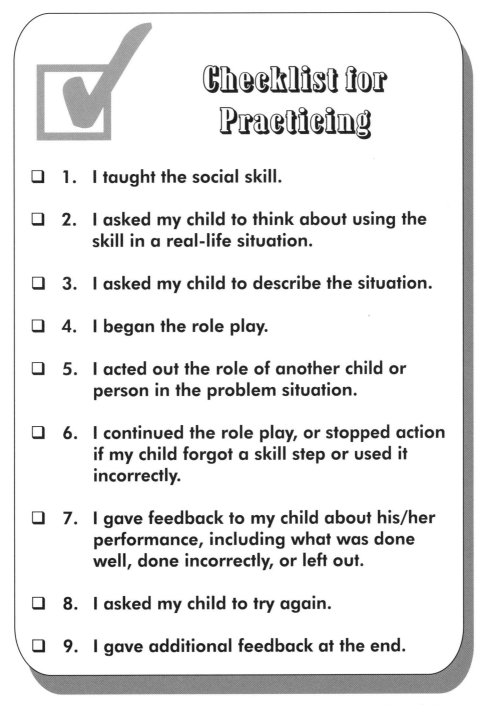

Checklist for Practicing

☐ 1. I taught the social skill.

☐ 2. I asked my child to think about using the skill in a real-life situation.

☐ 3. I asked my child to describe the situation.

☐ 4. I began the role play.

☐ 5. I acted out the role of another child or person in the problem situation.

☐ 6. I continued the role play, or stopped action if my child forgot a skill step or used it incorrectly.

☐ 7. I gave feedback to my child about his/her performance, including what was done well, done incorrectly, or left out.

☐ 8. I asked my child to try again.

☐ 9. I gave additional feedback at the end.

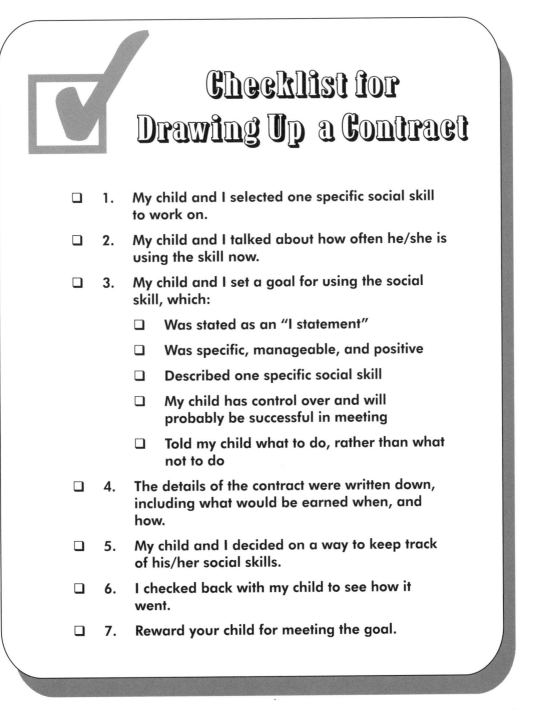

Checklist for Drawing Up a Contract

- ❑ 1. My child and I selected one specific social skill to work on.
- ❑ 2. My child and I talked about how often he/she is using the skill now.
- ❑ 3. My child and I set a goal for using the social skill, which:
    - ❑ Was stated as an "I statement"
    - ❑ Was specific, manageable, and positive
    - ❑ Described one specific social skill
    - ❑ My child has control over and will probably be successful in meeting
    - ❑ Told my child what to do, rather than what not to do
- ❑ 4. The details of the contract were written down, including what would be earned when, and how.
- ❑ 5. My child and I decided on a way to keep track of his/her social skills.
- ❑ 6. I checked back with my child to see how it went.
- ❑ 7. Reward your child for meeting the goal.

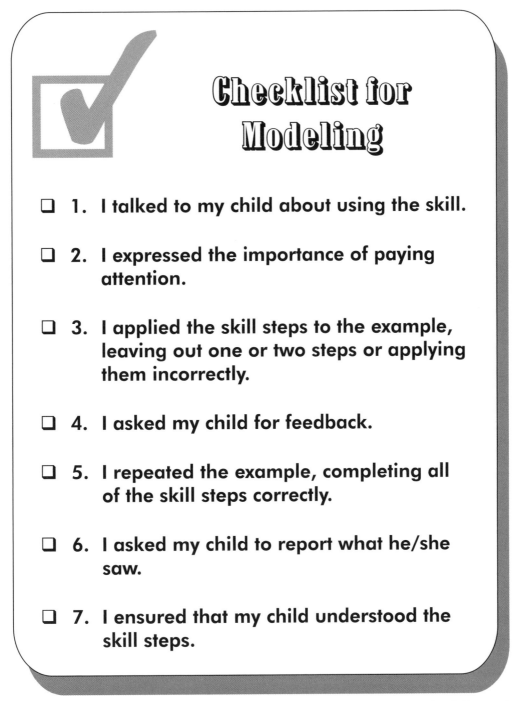

Checklist for Modeling

- ❑ 1. I talked to my child about using the skill.

- ❑ 2. I expressed the importance of paying attention.

- ❑ 3. I applied the skill steps to the example, leaving out one or two steps or applying them incorrectly.

- ❑ 4. I asked my child for feedback.

- ❑ 5. I repeated the example, completing all of the skill steps correctly.

- ❑ 6. I asked my child to report what he/she saw.

- ❑ 7. I ensured that my child understood the skill steps.

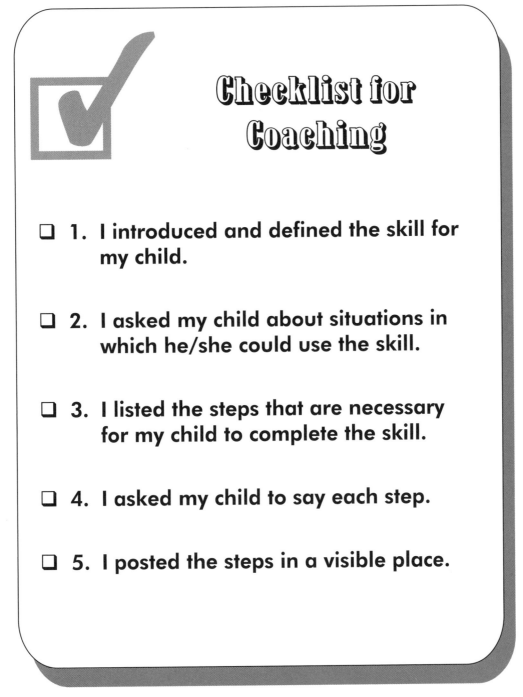

Checklist for Coaching

- ❑ 1. I introduced and defined the skill for my child.

- ❑ 2. I asked my child about situations in which he/she could use the skill.

- ❑ 3. I listed the steps that are necessary for my child to complete the skill.

- ❑ 4. I asked my child to say each step.

- ❑ 5. I posted the steps in a visible place.

Social Skills Chart

Social Skill/Behavior Being Observed: _____

Activity Being Observed: _____

Was the Skill/ Behavior Observed? [1]		What Happened? [2]
Yes	**No**	

NOTES:

1 = When you see an opportunity for your child to use a specific social skill or behavior, make a check in the Yes or No column. Check the "Yes" column each time your child demonstrates the social skill or behavior. Check the "No" column when your child has an opportunity to use a social skill, but fails to do so or demonstrates the skill inappropriately.

2 = Make notes in this space about the situation, such as who was present, what occurred before and after the skill or behavior, and other important details.

My Tally Chart

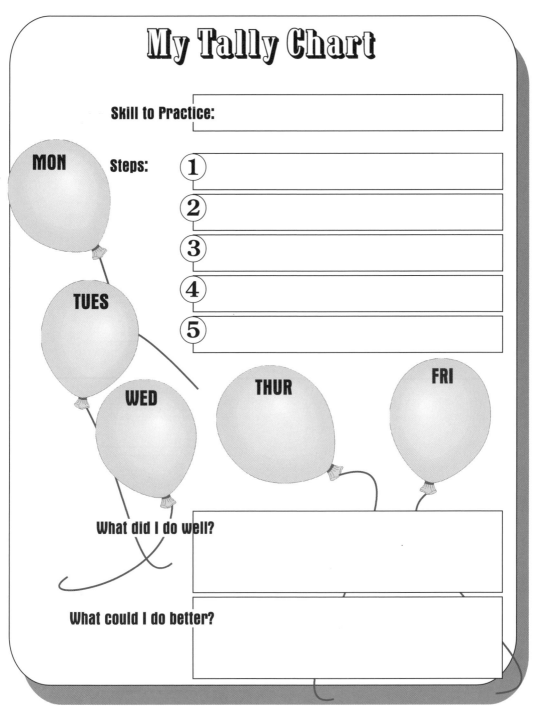

Skill to Practice:

MON

Steps:

1

2

3

4

5

TUES

WED

THUR

FRI

What did I do well?

What could I do better?

References

Colton, D.L. & Sheridan, S.M. (in press). Conjoint behavioral consultation and social skills training: Enhancing the play behavior of boys with attention deficit-hyperactivity disorder. *Journal of Educational and Psychological Consultation*.

Doll, B., Sheridan, S.M., & Law, M. (1990). *Friendship group: Parents manual*. Unpublished manuscript, University of Wisconsin-Madison, Department of Educational Psychology, Madison, WI.

Gordon, T. (1970). *P.E.T.: Parent effectiveness training: The tested new way to raise responsible children*. New York: Peter H. Wyden, Inc.

Jenson, W.R., Rhode, G., & Reavis, H.K. (1994). *The tough kid tool box*. Longmont, CO: Sopris West.

Jones, R., Sheridan, S.M., & Binns, W. (1993). School-wide social skills training: Providing preventive services to students at-risk. *School Psychology Quarterly, 8*, 57-80.

Rhode, G., Jenson, W.R., & Reavis, H.K. (1992). *The tough kid book*. Longmont, CO: Sopris West.

Sheridan, S.M. (1995). *The tough kid social skills book*. Longmont, CO: Sopris West.

Sheridan, S.M. & Dee, C.C. (1993). *Helping parents help kids: A manual for helping parents deal with children's social difficulties*. Unpublished manuscript, University of Utah, Department of Educational Psychology, Salt Lake City, UT.

Sheridan, S.M., Dee, C.C., Morgan, J., McCormick, M., & Walker, D. (1996). A multimethod intervention for social skills deficits in children with ADHD and their parents. *School Psychology Review*, *25*, 57-76.

Sheridan, S.M., Kratochwill, T.R., & Elliott, S.N. (1990). Behavioral consultation with parents and teachers: Delivering treatment for socially withdrawn children at home and school. *School Psychology Review*, *19*, 33-52.

Spivack, G. & Shure, M.B. (1974). *Social adjustment of young children: A cognitive approach to solving real life problems*. San Francisco: Jossey-Bass.

Weissberg, R.P., Gesten, E.L., Liebenstein, N.L., Doherty-Schmid, K., & Hutton, H. (1980). *The Rochester social problem-solving (SPS) program. A training manual for teachers of 2nd-4th grade*. Rochester, NY: University of Rochester.

Other Books of Interest From Sopris West

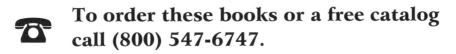

To order these books or a free catalog call (800) 547-6747.

Paraprofessionals As Reading Tutors

(formerly Parents As Reading Tutors)

Steven F. Duvall, Joseph C. Delquadri, and R. Vance Hall

In order to develop good reading skills, students must be given opportunities to practice reading. But many students, especially those with reading difficulties, need more practice than classroom time permits. This clear, easy-to-use guide presents a simple process paraprofessionals or family members can use to provide the additional reading practice children may need.

Based on ten years of research, the proven procedure in Paraprofessionals As Reading Tutors is easy to learn and requires only 11-15 minutes of tutoring per day. No additional training is needed; the tutoring sessions can be conducted at home without any additional materials. The procedure can also be used with students of any age.

The simple procedure increases reading speed, comprehension, and test scores for a wide range of students—from those with learning disabilities to those who simply need more reading practice. It also helps good readers to improve their reading comprehension. Included are ways to develop children's independent reading skills as well as tips for encouraging them to read for enjoyment. 32 pages.

From the Homework Partners Series
Practical Strategies for Parents and Teachers
William Jenson, Daniel Olympia, Debra Andrews, Julie Bowen, Lane Valum, and Melanie Hepworth-Neville

Sanity Savers for Parents: Tips for Tackling Homework

Sanity Savers does not suggest that parents become their children's teacher or spend endless time supervising their homework. Instead, ideas to support the effective homework program implemented in the classroom are provided. Sanity Savers teaches parents, through five self-directed weekly sessions, techniques to identify their children's homework problems and solve them easily. Focus is on the home study environment, commitment to daily study, scheduling and self-management by the student, troubleshooting common problems, and the Home Note system. 66 pages.

Study Buddies: Parent Tutoring Tactics

In addition to assistance with homework, parent tutoring ensures that children receive individual and consistent practice on academic skills critical for success. Designed to teach parents how to be effective tutors to their children at home, Study Buddies includes tutoring instructions for basic facts in reading, math, and spelling as well as fun techniques for motivating their children and monitoring their progress. Each approach uses research-validated procedures of teaching, presented in an easy to read format free from technical jargon. 124 pages.

Reaching Out to Today's Kids
15 Helpful Ways to Bridge the Gap Between Parents, Teachers, and Kids
(formerly Reaching Out to Troubled Kids)
Kathleen McConnell, Susie Kelly Flatau

Break the cycle of negative communication with your kids. This "quick read" for parents and teachers offers communication-builders that are both genuine and easy to do. Fifteen brief chapters help you create and maintain positive, open relationships with youths. You'll learn how to mesh expectations and social skills with the deeper feelings that affect relationships. Plus, the new format for this edition allows space for you to write your own thoughts and reflections as you grow your communication skills. 116 pages.

The Tough Kid Social Skills Book
Part of the "Tough Kid" series by Rhode, Jenson, and Reavis
Susan M. Sheridan

Employing many of the same successful strategies utilized in the rest of the "Tough Kid" series, *The Tough Kid Social Skills Book* offers detailed, specific methods for teachers, school psychologists, counselors, social workers, and school support staff to identify and assess "Tough Kids," and provides effective techniques for turning these kids around.

The Tough Kid Social Skills Book is conveniently divided into two sections. Part I provides the theoretical background and practical strategies for maximizing the effectiveness of a social skills program. Included are social skills training principles; multi-gating assessments/evaluation procedures; and tactics for structuring social skills group interventions, including modeling and role playing. Part II presents practitioners with flexible outlines—each structured to be completed in less than 60 minutes—for conducting social skills sessions. Included are skills in social entry, maintaining interactions, and problem-solving. 230 pages.

Social Skills Card
1

Body Basics

STEPS OF FEVER:

1. **F**ACE the other person.
2. Use **E**YE contact.
3. Use an appropriate **V**OICE.
4. Watch **E**XPRESSIONS.
5. Use the **R**IGHT posture and Relax.

DO

▶ Remember FEVER.
▶ Smile.
▶ Count to five or ten if you need to relax.
▶ Use friendly words.
▶ Take a deep breath before talking.
▶ Stay in your own space.

DON'T

▶ Stare at the other person.
▶ Look at your feet or somewhere else.
▶ Get too close or too far.
▶ Mumble your words or slouch.
▶ Clench your fists or jaw.

- cut along dotted line -

Social Skills Card
2

Conversation

STEPS:

1. Use Body Basics (FEVER).
2. Greet the other person (say "hi" and use their name).
3. Decide what to say (ask a question, give a compliment, or talk about something in common).
4. Wait for the right time.

DO

▶ Remember FEVER.
▶ Smile.
▶ Take a deep breath before talking.
▶ Use friendly words.

DON'T

▶ Yell or whisper.
▶ Interrupt the other person if he/she is talking or working.
▶ Use inappropriate words.
▶ Get into the other person's space.

What are Body Basics?

▶ Actions or behaviors we use that send messages to others, sometimes without even using words.

▶ Things we do with our face and bodies while we are talking to or playing with others.

▶ Important body signs that can be remembered with the word FEVER: Face the other person, use Eye contact, use the right Voice, watch Expressions, use the Right body posture and Relax.

Why is it important to use good Body Basics? In what situations would you use this skill?

▶ To let others know you like them or are interested in what they are saying or doing.

▶ To help yourself feel confident when interacting with or talking to others.

Let's pretend that I want to ask my teacher for permission to get a book from my locker. This is what I would do. Watch closely and tell me which Body Basics I use and which I forget.

▶ Show your child FEVER by remembering all of the steps or forgetting some.

▶ Ask your child what you did well and what you could do better.

▶ Ask for feedback about the specific steps of FEVER.

Now pretend that you want to ask your teacher for some help with a math problem. Go through the steps of Body Basics (FEVER).

▶ Practice FEVER with your child, watching what he/she does to use the steps.

▶ Have your child practice again, until all the skill steps are followed correctly.

▶ Ask your child when this skill can be used at school or other places.

- cut along dotted line -

What does it mean to start a conversation?

▶ To begin talking to someone who you aren't already talking to.

▶ To start talking about something you want to talk about.

▶ To ask questions if you need an answer.

Why is it important to know how to start a conversation? In what situations would you use this skill?

▶ You might want to play with or talk to the person.

▶ You might need to have a question answered.

Let's pretend that I want to tell my friend about a new puppy that I got. This is what I would do. Watch closely and tell me which steps I use and which steps I forget.

▶ Demonstrate the steps of starting a conversation by remembering all of the steps or forgetting some.

▶ Ask your child what you did well and what you could do better.

▶ Ask for feedback about the specific steps of starting a conversation.

Now pretend that you want to tell your friend about a movie you went to. Go through the steps of starting a conversation.

▶ Practice starting a conversation with your child, watching what he/she does to follow the steps.

▶ Tell your child what was done well and what to work on.

▶ Have your child practice until all the skill steps are followed correctly.

▶ Ask your child when this skill can be used at school or other places.

Social Skills Card
3

Joining In

STEPS:

1. Use Body Basics (FEVER).
2. Greet the other person.
3. Wait for the right time.
4. Ask to join ("Can I join you?" or "Can I play too?").

 **DO**   **DON'T**

DO	DON'T
▶ Remember the Body Basics.	▶ Yell or whisper.
▶ Smile.	▶ Interrupt the other person.
▶ Use friendly words.	▶ Use inappropriate words.
	▶ Get too close or too far from the other person.

------------------------------ cut along dotted line ------------------------------

Social Skills Card
4

Noticing and Talking About Feelings

STEPS:

1. Use Body Basics (FEVER).
2. Decide how you feel or how the other person feels (refer to body cues).
3. Wait for the right time (make sure the person is able to listen, and don't interrupt).
4. Say how you feel, or ask the other person how he or she feels (start with "I" statements, such as "I feel…" and "I think…").

 DO   **DON'T**

DO	DON'T
▶ Remember the Body Basics.	▶ Yell or scream.
▶ Stay calm and relaxed.	▶ Lose your cool.
▶ Take a deep breath before talking.	▶ Blame others for your feelings.
▶ Use "I" statements, such as "I feel…".	

What does it mean to join in?
- To play with others who are already playing a game.
- To do something with a group of other children.

Coach

Why is it important to know how to join in? In what situations would you use this skill?
- To be able to play with others.
- To have fun with a group of children.
- To become a part of a group.

Model

Let's pretend that I want to walk home from school with two girls who live in the neighborhood. This is what I would do. Watch closely and tell me which steps I use and which steps I forget.
- Show your child the steps of joining in by remembering all the steps or forgetting some.
- Ask your child what you did well and what you could do better.
- Ask about the skill steps and Body Basics.

Practice

Now pretend that you see me and another child eating lunch together and you want to eat with us. Go through the steps of joining in.
- Practice joining in with your child, watching what he/she does to follow the steps.
- Tell your child what was done well and what to work on.
- Have your child practice until all the skill steps are followed correctly.
- Ask your child when this skill can be used at school or other places.

------------------------------ cut along dotted line ------------------------------

What does it mean to notice and express feelings?
- To be able to tell how you are feeling, or how someone else might be feeling.
- To be able to talk about how you are feeling using feeling words.
- To understand body cues, facial cues, and voice tone.

Coach

Why is it important to notice how you feel or how others feel? In what situations would you use this skill?
- It can help us understand ourselves/the other person.
- To show the other person that we care about them.
- So that others know how we feel.
- To let others understand our feelings and treat us nicer.
- So our feelings don't get stored up inside and cause us to hurt inside.
- So our feelings don't come out in a way that we don't want.

Model

Let's pretend that I want to tell my friend that I was disappointed when I wasn't invited to her party. This is what I would do. Watch closely and tell me which steps I use and which steps I forget.
- Demonstrate noticing and talking about feelings by remembering all of the steps or forgetting some.
- Ask your child what you did well and what you could do better.
- Ask for feedback about the specific steps of noticing and talking about feelings.

Practice

Now pretend that you want to tell your friend that you were hurt when your classmates were joking about your new haircut. Go through the steps.
- Practice noticing and talking about feelings with your child, watching what he/she does to follow the steps.
- Tell your child what was done well and what to work on.
- Have your child practice until all the skill steps are followed correctly.
- Ask your child when this skill can be used at school or other places.

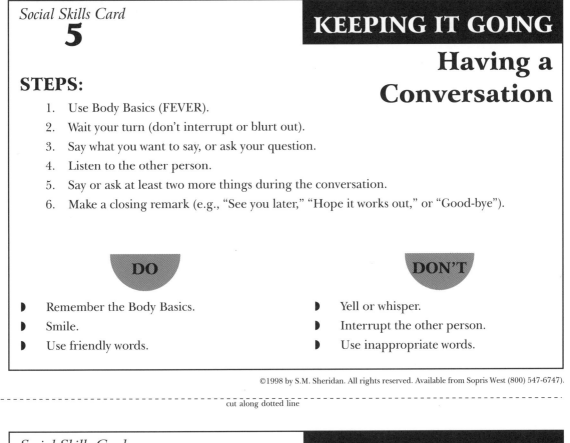

Social Skills Card
5

STEPS:

1. Use Body Basics (FEVER).
2. Wait your turn (don't interrupt or blurt out).
3. Say what you want to say, or ask your question.
4. Listen to the other person.
5. Say or ask at least two more things during the conversation.
6. Make a closing remark (e.g., "See you later," "Hope it works out," or "Good-bye").

DO

▶ Remember the Body Basics.
▶ Smile.
▶ Use friendly words.

DON'T

▶ Yell or whisper.
▶ Interrupt the other person.
▶ Use inappropriate words.

- cut along dotted line -

Social Skills Card
6

STEPS:

1. Use Body Basics (FEVER).
2. Decide who starts (read the directions, flip a coin, roll a die).
3. Wait your turn.
4. Talk and listen to the other person (have a conversation).

DO

▶ Smile.
▶ Use friendly words.
▶ Look at the directions if you don't know them.

DON'T

▶ Yell, whisper, or use inappropriate words.
▶ Argue about the rules of the game.
▶ Be a sore loser.

Coach

What does it mean to have a conversation?
- To spend time with a person talking.
- To talk about school, movies, sports, or something you both like or that you have in common, etc.

Why is it important to know how to have a conversation? In what situations would you use this skill?
- To be able to talk to others.
- To tell others something important.
- To find out something from others.

Model

Let's pretend that I want to tell my brother about what I did in school today. This is what I would do. Watch closely and tell me which steps I use and which steps I forget.
- Show your child the steps of having a conversation by remembering all of the steps or forgetting some.
- Ask your child what you did well and what you could do better.
- Ask for feedback about the specific steps of having a conversation.

Practice

Now pretend that you want to tell your friend about a new toy you got. Go through the steps of having a conversation.
- Practice having a conversation with your child, watching what he/she does to follow the steps.
- Tell your child what was done well and what to work on.
- Have your child practice until all the skill steps are followed correctly.
- Ask your child when this skill can be used at school or other places.

- cut along dotted line -

Coach

What does it mean to play cooperatively?
- To play together in a fair way.
- To share, take turns, and help each other.

Why is it important to know how to play cooperatively? In what situations would you use this skill?
- So everyone knows what to do.
- To be able to get along when playing.
- To make the game more fun.

Model

Let's pretend that I am playing a game of cards with my friend. This is what I would do. Watch closely and tell me which steps I use and which steps I forget.
- Show your child the steps of playing cooperatively by remembering all of the steps or forgetting some.
- Ask your child what you did well and what you could do better.
- Ask for feedback about the specific steps of playing cooperatively.

Practice

Now pretend that you are playing checkers with your friend. Go through the steps of playing cooperatively.
- Practice playing cooperatively with your child, watching what he/she does to follow the steps.
- Tell your child what was done well and what to work on.
- Have your child practice until all the skill steps are followed correctly.
- Ask your child when this skill can be used at school or other places.

Social Skills Card

7

SOLVING PROBLEMS

STEPS:

1. Stop, take a deep breath, and count to five.
2. Decide what the problem is and how you feel.
3. Think about your choices and their consequences.
4. Decide on your best choice.
5. Do it.

 DO

 DON'T

DO	DON'T
◗ Remember the Body Basics.	◗ Yell, scream, or use inappropriate words.
◗ Relax.	◗ Call the other person names.
◗ Tell yourself to be calm.	◗ Hit or kick the other person.
◗ Think of at least three choices.	◗ Use "they" statements.
◗ Use "I" statements.	

--- cut along dotted line ---

Social Skills Card

8

SOLVING PROBLEMS
Controlling Anger

STEPS:

1. Stop, take a deep breath, and count to five.
2. Decide what the problem is and how you feel.
3. Think about your choices and their consequences (emphasize positive choices).
4. Decide on your best choice.

 DO

 DON'T

DO	DON'T
◗ Remember the Body Basics.	◗ Yell, scream, or use inappropriate words.
◗ Relax.	◗ Call the other person names.
◗ Tell yourself to be calm and that it's OK.	◗ Hit or kick.
◗ Talk calmly.	
◗ Compromise.	
◗ Think of at least three choices.	

Coach

What does it mean to solve problems?
- ▶ To use steps to deal with problems when they occur.
- ▶ To know how to act or behave when there is a problem with others.

Why is it important to solve problems? In what situations would you use this skill?
- ▶ To keep friends.
- ▶ To get along better with friends, parents, and others.
- ▶ To know how to deal with problems when they come up.

Model

Let's pretend that I am watching my favorite TV show and my sister comes into the room and changes the channel. This is what I would do. Watch closely and tell me which steps I use and which steps I forget.
- ▶ Demonstrate the steps of solving problems by remembering all of the steps or forgetting some. Indicate what you are thinking about the problem, choices, and consequences by whispering the thoughts.
- ▶ Ask your child what you did well and what you could do better.
- ▶ Ask for feedback about the specific steps of solving problems.

Practice

Now pretend that you are reading a book and a friend takes it from you. Go through the steps of solving problems.
- ▶ Practice solving problems with your child, watching what he/she does to follow the steps.
- ▶ Tell your child what was done well and what to work on.
- ▶ Have your child practice until all skill steps are followed correctly.
- ▶ Ask your child when this skill can be used at school or other places.

-------------------------------- cut along dotted line --------------------------------

Coach

What does it mean to use self control?
- ▶ To remain calm when you get angry, disappointed, frustrated, or when you don't get your way.
- ▶ To keep from getting into fights.

Why is it important to use self-control? In what situations would you use this skill?
- ▶ To get along with others.
- ▶ To stay out of trouble.
- ▶ To feel better about yourself.
- ▶ To solve problems calmly and to keep friends.

Model

Let's pretend that my mom says I cannot watch a video because I did not clean my room. This is what I would do. Watch closely and tell me which steps I use and which steps I forget.
- ▶ Show your child the steps of controlling anger by remembering all of the steps or forgetting some.
- ▶ Ask your child what you did well and what you could do better.
- ▶ Ask for feedback about the specific steps of controlling anger.

Practice

Now pretend that you are at school and someone took your new soccer ball. Go through the steps of controlling anger.
- ▶ Practice controlling anger with your child, watching what he/she does to follow the steps.
- ▶ Tell your child what was done well and what to work on.
- ▶ Have your child practice until all the skill steps are followed correctly.
- ▶ Ask your child when this skill can be used at school or other places.

Social Skills Card
9

SOLVING PROBLEMS
Arguments

STEPS:

1. Stop, take a deep breath, and count to five.
2. Decide what the problem is and how you feel.
3. Think about your choices and their consequences.
4. Decide on your best choice.
5. Do it.

DO

▸ Remember the Body Basics.
▸ Compromise.
▸ Tell yourself to be calm and that it's OK.
▸ Think of at least three positive choices to solve the fight.

DON'T

▸ Yell, scream, or use inappropriate words.
▸ Call the other person names.
▸ Hit, kick, or argue with the other person.

- cut along dotted line -

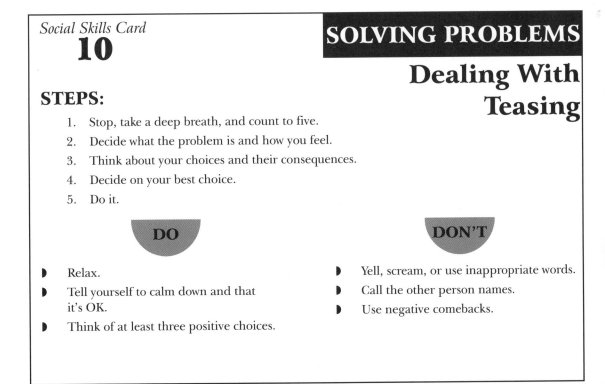

Social Skills Card
10

SOLVING PROBLEMS
Dealing With Teasing

STEPS:

1. Stop, take a deep breath, and count to five.
2. Decide what the problem is and how you feel.
3. Think about your choices and their consequences.
4. Decide on your best choice.
5. Do it.

DO

▸ Relax.
▸ Tell yourself to calm down and that it's OK.
▸ Think of at least three positive choices.

DON'T

▸ Yell, scream, or use inappropriate words.
▸ Call the other person names.
▸ Use negative comebacks.

Coach

What does it mean to solve arguments?
- ❯ To stop an argument before it gets too bad.
- ❯ To use self-control when in an argument.

Why is it important to solve fights and arguments?
In what situations would you use this skill?
- ❯ To get along better with others.
- ❯ To keep friends.

Model

Let's pretend that my friend and I disagree about the rules of a new game. This is what I would do. Watch closely and tell me which steps I use and which steps I forget.
- ❯ Demonstrate solving arguments by remembering all of the steps or forgetting some.
- ❯ Ask your child what you did well and what you could do better.
- ❯ Ask for feedback about the specific steps of solving arguments.

Practice

Now pretend that your teacher wants you to clean the chalkboards even though you just did it yesterday. Go through the steps of solving arguments.
- ❯ Practice solving arguments with your child, watching what he/she does to follow the steps.
- ❯ Tell your child what was done well and what to work on.
- ❯ Have your child practice until all skill steps are followed correctly.
- ❯ Ask your child when this skill can be used at school or other places.

- cut along dotted line -

Coach

What does it mean to deal with teasing?
- ❯ To handle situations when other kids make fun of something you say or do.
- ❯ To keep from losing control when someone bothers you.

Why is it important to deal with teasing? In what situations would you use this skill?
- ❯ To remain in control and not let others "push your buttons."
- ❯ To feel good about yourself even if someone is trying to make you mad.
- ❯ To be able to think good things about yourself.

Model

Let's pretend that some children at school are teasing me because I got new glasses. This is what I would do. Watch closely and tell me which steps I use and which steps I forget.
- ❯ Demonstrate dealing with teasing by remembering all of the steps or forgetting some.
- ❯ Ask your child what you did well and what you could do better.
- ❯ Ask for feedback about the specific steps of dealing with teasing.

Practice

Now pretend that some of your classmates are teasing you about making mistakes on homework. Go through the steps of dealing with teasing.
- ❯ Practice dealing with teasing with your child, watching what he/she does to follow the steps.
- ❯ Tell your child what was done well and what to work on.
- ❯ Have your child practice until all the skill steps are followed correctly.
- ❯ Ask your child when this skill can be used at school or other places.

Social Skills Card
11

Dealing With
Being Left Out

STEPS:

1. Stop, take a deep breath, and count to five.
2. Decide what the problem is and how you feel.
3. Think about choices and their consequences.
4. Decide on your best choice.
5. Do it.

 DO

 DON'T

- Relax.
- Use Body Basics.
- Tell yourself to be calm and that it's OK.
- Think good thoughts about yourself.

- Pout.
- Call other people names.
- Interrupt other people.

- cut along dotted line -

Social Skills Card
12

Accepting "No"

STEPS:

1. Stop, take a deep breath, and count to five.
2. Decide what the problem is and how you feel.
3. Think about your choices and their consequences.
4. Decide on your best choice.
5. Do it.

DO

DON'T

- Relax.
- Tell yourself to be calm.
- Tell yourself that it's OK.

- Pout, whine, or beg.
- Talk back.
- Yell at the other person.

Coach

What does it mean to deal with being left out?
- To stay in control when other kids leave you out of games and activities that you want to be part of.
- To think positive things when everyone else is doing something and you are not included.

Why is it important to deal with being left out? In what situations would you use this skill?
- To remain in control if you don't get invited or included.
- To feel good about yourself even if you're not included.
- To be able to think good things about yourself.

Model

Let's pretend that I was the last in your class chosen to be on a softball team. This is what I would do. Watch closely and tell me which steps I use and which steps I forget.
- Demonstrate dealing with being left out by remembering all of the steps or forgetting some.
- Ask your child what you did well and what you could do better.
- Ask for feedback about the specific steps of being left out.

Practice

Now pretend that you didn't get invited to a classmate's birthday party. Go through the steps of dealing with being left out.
- Practice dealing with being left out with your child, watching what he/she does to follow the steps.
- Tell your child what was done well and what to work on.
- Have your child practice until all skill steps are followed correctly.
- Ask your child when this skill can be used at school or other places.

-- cut along dotted line --

Coach

What does it mean to accept "no"?
- To stay in control when you want something that you cannot have (such as extra money or a special privilege).
- To remain calm when you want to do something that you cannot do (such as spend the night at a friend's house or have extra time to do an assignment).

Why is it important to accept "no"? In what situations would you use this skill?
- So other people can count on you to understand and not react negatively.

Model

Let's pretend that my teacher told me I could not work on the computer, but I *really* want to. This is what I would do. Watch closely and tell me which steps I use and which steps I forget.
- Demonstrate accepting "no" by remembering all of the steps or forgetting some.
- Ask your child what you did well and what you could do better.
- Ask for feedback about the specific steps of accepting "no".

Practice

Now pretend that your friend says that you cannot play with him at recess. Go through the steps of accepting "no".
- Practice accepting "no" with your child, watching what he/she does to follow the steps.
- Tell your child what was done well and what to work on.
- Have your child practice until all the skill steps are followed correctly.
- Ask your child when this skill can be used at school or other places.